ALSO BY PETER WALSH

How to Organize (Just About) Everything:

More Than 500 Step-by-Step Instructions

for Everything from Organizing Your Closets

to Planning a Wedding to Creating

a Flawless Filing System

It's All Too
MUCH

*An Easy Plan
for Living a Richer Life
with Less Stuff*

PETER WALSH

FREE PRESS
New York   London   Toronto   Sydney

To KRG—for the basic premise

FREE PRESS
A Division of Simon & Schuster, Inc.
1230 Avenue of the Americas
New York, NY 10020

First Free Press trade paperback edition December 2007

FREE PRESS and colophon are trademarks of Simon & Schuster, Inc.

For information regarding special discounts for bulk purchases,
please contact Simon & Schuster Special Sales at
1-800-456-6798 or business@simonandschuster.com

Designed by Katy Riegel

Manufactured in the United States of America

17   19   20   18   16

The Library of Congress has cataloged the hardcover edition as follows:
Walsh, Peter.
It's all too much : an easy plan for living a richer life
with less stuff / Peter Walsh.
p.   cm.
1. Storage in the home.   2. Orderliness.   3. House cleaning.   I. Title.
TX309 . W34 2007
640—dc22   2006049195

ISBN-13: 978-0-7432-9264-1
ISBN-10: 0-7432-9264-2
ISBN-13: 978-0-7432-9265-8 (pbk)
ISBN-10: 0-7432-9265-0 (pbk)

Contents

The things you own end up owning you.

—*FIGHT CLUB*

Introduction

SOMETHING IS AFOOT. Something that until recently I could not have imagined or predicted. Something that is changing the basic fabric of people's lives and is impacting how all of us relate to the things we have and the things we own. Something that affects us all. We are, as a nation, overwhelmed with too much stuff.

Did the title of this book catch your eye? Maybe you are at a stage in your life where something in your life is too much—your career, your relationship, or "just everything" is suddenly overwhelming. If so, you are part of a harsh awakening in this country, and across much of the developed world, as we come to realize that happiness and success might not be measured by more material things. That having more possessions may be more suffocating than liberating. That a larger house, better car, and more "stuff" come with no guarantee of greater happiness. That for many of us, the stuff we own ends up owning us. Suddenly you look around at the life you've built and all you've acquired and realize that it's all too much!

I have an unusual job. I help people dig themselves out from under the overwhelming crush of their own possessions. I'm not talking about a messy closet or one too many boxes of holiday decorations in the garage. I work with people who have filled their homes, their offices, sometimes their cars, and always their lives with too much stuff. These are people who have lost the ability to deal reasonably and rationally with what they own. They fill every corner of their homes with clothes, papers, their kids' school projects, wrapping paper, collectibles, scrapbooking materials, garden tools, kitchen products, sporting gear, antiques, dolls, toys, books, car parts, and every imaginable (and unimaginable!) item you could list.

Surprisingly, as I've traveled across the United States helping people declutter and get organized, I have come to see that the problem is one that affects far more families than I could have imagined. Every single person I have met tells me not only about their own clutter problem, but the clutter problems of a family member, or those of a friend. Nobody seems immune. The stories are not dissimilar—papers and magazines run amok, garages overflow with unopened boxes, kids' toys fill rooms, and closets are so stuffed that it looks like the clothing department of a major retailer is having a fire sale. The epidemic of clutter, the seeming inability to get organized, and the sense that "the stuff" is taking over affects us all.

We are at the center of an orgy of consumption, and many are now seeing that this need to own so much comes with a heavy price: Kids so overstimulated by the sheer volume of stuff in their home that they lose the ability to concentrate and focus. Financial strain caused by misplaced bills or overpurchasing. Constant fighting because neither partner is prepared to let go of their possessions. The embarrassment of living in a house that long ago became more of a storage facility than a home.

This clutter doesn't just come in the form of the physical

items that crowd our homes. We are bombarded every day with dire predictions of disaster and face many uncertainties—some real and many manufactured. Think about the perils that we've been warned about in the last decade alone—killer bees, Y2K, SARS, anthrax, mad cow disease, avian flu, flesh-eating bacteria . . . the list goes on and on. We are also faced daily with reports of war, an unstable economy, and global terrorism coming very close to home. Surprisingly, this endless barrage (its own kind of clutter) inspires many of the families with whom I work to finally take control of their own clutter. In an unpredictable, dangerous world that is out of their control, they look to their homes for stability—to get some degree of organization back into their closets, their garages, their home offices, their lives. This quest for organization is a deeply personal response to the feeling that the rest of the world is out of control.

Among the clutter, the frustration, and the yearning for organization, I constantly hear the same refrain: It is all overwhelming. The stuff has taken on a life of its own and families have no idea where to even begin. They are paralyzed by their own stuff. Often the people I work with lament, "It's all too much—help me!"

If you find yourself at the point of being overwhelmed by your possessions, you have a clear choice: Decide here and now that you no longer want your stuff to overrun your life. Work with me to get balance and harmony back into your family and relationships. It can be done and I know how. None of this frightens me or overwhelms me because I have seen it all. I have never walked away from a cluttered home because it was too much. However, I *have* walked away from those who value their stuff over their relationships, their things over their dreams, or their possessions over their vision for the life they really want.

If you are one of those for whom it's suddenly all too much

and want to let go, come on an exciting journey with me to reclaim your life. Living a richer, fuller, more exciting, and rewarding life is not that far away. Trust me, I've led many there already and you can be next. I promise you, if you do this, there is nothing you can't do!

IT'S ALL TOO MUCH

Let me tell you about one of my average workdays. One sunny June day, Jared and Lisa invited me into their modest house in the suburbs of Maryland. From the tree-lined street their home looked welcoming. The grass was neatly trimmed, the garden in full bloom. A gray sedan was parked in the driveway. I rang the doorbell.

The door opened to an appalling site. The floor was invisible. Every flat surface was stacked high with papers. The walls were lined with wall-to-wall file boxes, some stacked on shelves or tables. Many of the piles reached the top of my head and I'm not a short man. The living room was so crowded that the kitchen had become their little boy Cooper's playroom. A toy train track ran through the legs of the kitchen table, its cars long ago scattered, tripped on, and lost. The family was overrun with what appeared to be scrapbooking materials: glue, notebooks, piles of photos, trim, and all sorts of craft material. In short, the house was a disaster. I glanced at Jared and Lisa. To all appearances they are clean, hardworking, upstanding citizens, no different from you or me. Jared manages a successful airport shuttle business. After taking a few years off to have their first child, Lisa has just gotten her real-estate license. Cooper was three years old and delighted in showing me his firm handshake. A great family. And a successful one, in spite of the clutter. But underneath their sunny exterior was tension. They wanted more from their lives and believed the chaos of their home was taking away from their happiness. There was an obvious question that needed an answer: Why was their house completely out of control?

I asked Lisa what it was like living in this chaos. She said, "It's suffocating. I feel like I can't breathe when I look in the office." Lisa felt buried by her own stuff. She went on, "Something has to change. I don't want to live like this. But I have no idea where to begin."

And then I heard the one refrain that sums it all up, the words of despair that I hear over and over again from everyone I work with: "It's all too much."

That is why I decided to call this book *It's All Too Much*. It's a response to the hopelessness of that refrain. It's about what to do when you reach the point where you don't know where to start. When you're faced with so much mess that you throw up your hands in despair and give up. When you just want to move into a hotel, or throw it all out, or shove it in the garage, like when you were a kid and stuffed all your dirty clothes under the bed. Amazingly, I have dealt with people who have purchased a second home rather than face the mammoth task of decluttering the home they have lived in for many years! Well, there's no place to hide your mess when you're an adult and, eventually, you have to come home, so you might as well start dealing with the problem now. *It's All Too Much* is the solution.

It's just stuff

I asked Jared if he felt as overwhelmed as Lisa. He shrugged. "I know our house doesn't belong in *Martha Stewart*, but we're busy. It's just stuff. I don't see what the big deal is." I walked over to their bookshelf and started scanning the titles. There were diet books. Exercise books. Self-esteem books. Career motivation books. Parenting books. Finance books. Marriage books. Books on how to live better, happier, richer, fuller lives. It was a complete library of self-help books for every issue a family might have. It was time for me to tell him what I tell all of my clients: the truth. It was time to hold a mirror up to their life and their clutter so that they could see what was happening. I sat him and Lisa down and said, "You think the state of this house is no big deal, but look at all these problems you're trying to solve." I gestured toward the stack of self-help books. "Your home is the physical and emotional base for your family. You want to change? To get motivated? Improve your self-image? Lose weight? Start by taking a look at your home.

"You want a life built on a solid foundation, but you can't even see the floor beneath you. You want to lose weight, but your kitchen is overwhelmed with appliances you never use. You want to build your career, but your office literally makes you feel ill. You want change? This is where it starts: your home. Where you live, breathe, rest, love, and create. Forget the self-help books. Get rid of the clutter. Get organized. If you do, I promise that every aspect of your life will change in ways that you never imagined possible."

Jared and Lisa were like so many couples that I deal with— they had lost sight of the fact that who you are and what you have are intimately linked. The things you buy, the items you value, the possessions you hoard are all a reflection of you, your life, your relationships, your career, and your aspirations. You are not your stuff, but, believe me, your stuff reveals a great deal about who you are.

THIS MEANS YOU

Jared and Lisa did want to change. That's exactly why they called me. In 2003, I became the organization expert on a TV show called *Clean Sweep,* a series for the cable station TLC. The mission of each episode of *Clean Sweep* was clear: A team of experts had forty-eight hours to help a family get uncluttered and organized. It was a simple formula. We had two days and two thousand dollars to redo two clutter-ridden rooms of the family's home. I do the same thing for private clients like Jared and Lisa. But simple as the concept seems—getting rid of the stuff that overwhelms their homes—there's more to the problem than meets the eye.

Bear with me here as I walk you through Lisa and Jared's home. It may not look exactly like your house—you may make beaded jewelry or collect ancient pottery instead of scrapbooking—but I have a feeling you'll recognize bits and pieces of your own life in Jared and Lisa's. If I have learned one thing in this job, it's that when it comes to clutter, we are all far more similar than we think!

As Jared and Lisa finished showing me their house, Lisa turned to me and asked, "How did this happen? We work hard; we live in a nice neighborhood. Why us?" I looked out the window at the other houses up and down the street. From the outside they looked just like Jared and Lisa's. And I was willing to bet that they had the same problems behind those closed doors. The person for whom clutter is not an issue is rare. We are all in some way owned by our possessions. As we get older our families grow. Children outgrow their toys and their clothes. We accumulate books and papers. We take on new hobbies and collections. Our extended family members die and we inherit boxes—or truckloads—of their possessions. Stuff is cheap—look at electronics. Not too long ago, televisions and computers were big purchases that you only made a few times during your life. Now we think nothing of replacing them every couple of years or buying new ones rather than having them repaired.

The Container Store is a national chain—thirty-four stores and growing—selling storage and organization solutions, but, as their website boasts, there's no containing their growth. Their sales revenues grow 20 to 30 percent every year. Can you imagine if your possessions grew at that rate? This year The Container Store secured a new distribution center that's 65 percent bigger than the last to accommodate continued growth. Think about it: This is a store that sells only organizing solutions; that means that there are millions of Americans buying and trying to organize, but I guarantee there's very little organization as a result. And what's the typical American solution to having too much stuff? Buy another organization solution!

Then there are those of us who can't fit our belongings in containers and resort to self-storage, the no-man's-land of stuff. Self-storage is often supposed to be temporary—we'll just store this couch until we move to our next house, where we might have space for it—but it's a fifteen-billion-dollar industry. There are more than forty thousand self-storage facilities in this country, each averaging about fifty-five thousand square feet! This accumulation of stuff is a national trend. At some point, every one of us has to figure out how to manage this influx of stuff before it gets out of control.

FYI—SELF-STORAGE MANIA

The first self-storage facilities appeared in Texas in the late 1960s. Today, approximately 10 percent of American households have items in one of the forty thousand self-storage facilities in this country. This is a 75 percent increase from just ten years ago and it has happened during a time when the size of the average American house has increased by half. Larger houses *and* more stuff in storage!

Our home is too small

Before I could help Jared and Lisa get their clutter under control, I needed more information. What was all this stuff they owned? Where had it come from? How important was it to them? Why did they hold on to it?

We started with Lisa's scrapbooking materials. Truth be told, they were all over the house, but we started in their family room, scrapbooking headquarters. Lisa had taken up scrapbooking when Cooper was born. Her baby shower had a scrapbook theme, and it blossomed from there. There were photos, memorabilia, ribbons, stickers, and rubber stamps jockeying for space on her wraparound desk. The built-in bookshelves were stocked with labeled plastic storage bins, all so full that their lids floated inches above the bins. Lisa smiled weakly. "I know it looks bad, but I actually need all this stuff to do my albums. And I know where everything is. Almost."

Lisa didn't think that she was disorganized. There was a method behind the madness of that room. The real problem, as far as she was concerned, was that the room was too small. I agreed with her—but not on the size of the room. She was, indeed, organized, but she had organized an entire extra room's worth of stuff that wasn't necessary. We finally agreed that the problem wasn't that Lisa didn't have enough room; she simply had too much stuff. Instead of getting rid of some of it when she felt overwhelmed, Lisa just bought more storage systems (more stuff!). Who hasn't tried the same thing? At some time or another, we've all bought storage bins or file cabinets or a closet organizing system or invested in some other shiny new system that promises to elevate us to a higher plane of organization. In fact, I've found plenty of these very storage systems, still unused, wasting valuable space in people's garages, offices, and bedrooms. I am constantly amazed by the amount of stuff that people will squeeze into a room. Listen to me—it's a basic law of physics that you can't fit five cubic feet of stuff into three cubic feet of space! You cannot create more space than you have. Nevertheless, I know that people will keep on trying! Like I always say, rearrange the deck chairs on the *Titanic* as much as you want, the ship is still going down!

Meanwhile, Jared isn't sentimental like Lisa, but he is afraid of identity theft. He has saved every envelope or magazine that comes into the house with his name on it because he wants to make sure he shreds every single label to pulp. Jared's piles of paper and shredded strips completely overwhelmed their small office. While Jared's worry may be justified, the way he is dealing with the concern is creating a bigger, more immediate issue for his family that affects the way they live every day.

What's really important

Jared and Lisa couldn't just throw away their excess. For them, none of it was garbage because everything seemed important. Lisa had family photographs she wanted to arrange in albums for Cooper to pass down to his kids. Jared's office was full of materials he wanted for his company: employee records and business articles that he thought he'd get around to reading. How could they let go of any of it? This was all stuff that they would certainly need one day. "Fine," I said, "you have too much stuff, but you believe that all of it is critical to you. I understand. Instead of talking about the whole house, let's talk about the rooms one by one." They followed me into the family room. "What's the purpose of this room?" I asked Lisa.

"It's the family room. It's where I scrapbook and, well, Cooper's supposed to play in here, but he's always in the kitchen or the hall."

"I see. So what you're telling me is that hoarding photos for Cooper's future is more important to you than giving him room to play today?" I didn't wait for Lisa to answer. Jared was starting to gloat. He'd been down on Lisa's scrapbooking from the start, but I wasn't about to let him off easy. I went straight to the office.

"You're up, Jared."

"This is the office. I store my business papers here, pay bills, and we all use the computer."

"No you don't!" Lisa burst out. "You pay your bills standing up in the kitchen. When I'm trying to make dinner." She turned to me. "We almost had our electricity shut off because Jared lost the bill behind the stove."

I turned to Jared, "Is this true?" Jared nodded. "Because of the clutter in your office, some bills aren't getting paid. But you're still giving your paper shredding and business papers priority over paying bills and getting rid of the tension that it is causing between the two of you?"

"That's exactly what he's doing," Lisa said, shooting an apologetic look at Jared. "And I'm supposed to work from home. In that office? What a joke!" We went through every room of the house like this. I learned that Jared had every table-cloth his grandmother had owned stuffed in moldy cardboard boxes in the garage. He knew they were ruined, but he couldn't let them go. And Lisa was using the messy office as an excuse. She really wasn't sure if she wanted to go back to work or to take care of Cooper full-time. Their house reflected all of these con-flicts. But there was no way to resolve them until they could see what the real cost of keeping these "prized possessions" was to their family. They had to face some tough questions, answer them honestly, and decide on specific actions to change their situation.

IMAGINE THE LIFE YOU WANT

Once I understood the physical space and emotions behind Jared and Lisa's clutter, I told them that I wanted them to do an exercise that is fundamental to helping people declutter and get organized.

As I do with all my clients, I first asked Jared and Lisa to imagine their ideal lives. This is a question that always catches people off guard. They expect me to ask for an inventory of what they own, or a list of their collectibles, or even details of their home lives when they were children. My starting point, however, has nothing to do with "the stuff." I know it sounds strange, but if you start by focusing on the clutter, you will never get organized. Getting truly organized is rarely about "the stuff."

To get Jared and Lisa started, I gave them a little help. You're healthy, happy, and successful. Maybe you have a second child. Perhaps your family lives nearby—or all the way across the world. Your choice. You wake up in the morning feeling bright, energized, and ready to face the day. You know what you want— a rewarding career, a supportive community, minimal stress, a loving family, time to relax, and time to pursue your interests— and you've found a way to have it all.

"Yeah, right," Jared said.

Now I asked them to think about the lives they were actually living. Did the stuff they owned contribute to the lives they were hoping to achieve, or was it getting in the way of that vision? Jared said, "I want to be organized, efficient, and smart in how I use my time." Moments earlier I had watched him spend fifteen minutes trying to find his checkbook. He told me that he misplaced it several times a week. And Lisa had to admit that she couldn't really imagine launching her new work-from-home plan in a house that looked like this. This is the bottom line: If your stuff and the way it is organized is getting you to your goals . . . fantastic. But if it's impeding your vision for the life you want, then why is it in your home? Why is it in your life? Why do you cling to it? For me, this is the only starting point in dealing with clutter. These questions are the ultimate reality check when it comes to what you own and what you have in your home. The first step to getting organized is to work from the vision of the life you want to live. Everything flows from this.

In the eighteenth century, an English architect named William Morris wrote that you should not have anything in your home that is not beautiful or functional. A tough task. Your home is a metaphor for your life—it represents who you are and what you value. When your house is a wreck, your life starts to crumble. For Jared, who spent fifteen minutes twice a day looking for misplaced items, the cost of that activity alone was more than a week lost every year. That's not efficiency—that's lost opportunity!

You can't feel at peace when you're tripping over boxes of golf balls or struggling to find last month's electric bill. You can't have a happy family when you can't even see the dining table. For Jared and Lisa, the damage went beyond the overstuffed closets and overflowing desk drawers. They let stuff mess up their lives, their relationships, their priorities, their hopes, and, yes, their dreams—everything that should have been most important to them. Clutter had stopped them from living the lives they wished they had.

To a greater or lesser degree, I have seen this happen to hundreds of people. The stuff takes over. At some point there is a shift and suddenly life, love, family, and friends all take second place to the clutter. Think about the words we use when we talk about clutter. "There was so much stuff in that room I felt like I was *suffocating*," or "You should see that garage, you can *hardly breathe* in there with all those boxes," or "He is really *buried* under all that paperwork." We use these words for a specific reason—they aren't exaggerations. Clutter is insidious, a slow but steady tide. It enters your home little by little, usually over years. Clutter sucks life away. It leaves you depressed, overwhelmed, lacking motivation, and unable to breathe. Clutter prevents you from enjoying the most precious, intimate moments in life. Clutter robs you of far more than the space it occupies—it steals your life!

I told Lisa and Jared that if they wanted to change, they had to admit that lots of their "important stuff" wasn't as important as the space it was consuming. There was an absolute limit to what they should own and that limit was set by the space they had. Period. Their stuff exceeded the space they had to contain it reasonably, so it had started taking up the space they needed to live. Put another way, if they wanted to achieve the lives they envisioned for themselves, Lisa and Jared had to start redefining their relationship to their stuff. It may seem obvious, but—hard as some people try—you can't own everything! "Listen," I said to Lisa and Jared, "it's you or your stuff—make the choice!"

We started in the family room. Jared, Lisa, and I talked about their vision for the room. More than anything, they wanted a comfortable place to gather as a family. They wanted to have empty space for Cooper's play dates. They wanted a pleasant space to watch TV several nights a week. Lisa finally understood that she didn't need all the scrapbooking stuff she'd so assiduously acquired and organized when she actually spent more of her leisure time watching TV in a room cluttered with unused hobbies. So she made decisions about what to keep based on the space that she wanted to devote to the hobby. She agreed that half the bookshelves should be hers and half should be for Cooper's toys. She also agreed that she wouldn't keep any scrapbooking materials that didn't fit on her side of the bookshelves in closed bins. Jared proposed that she give up on scrapbooking any of their vacation photos. She gave him a gentle punch, but he didn't give in: "They're boring and you know it." Once we knew the vision, purpose, and goals for the room, we went through the whole mess, bin by bin, with Jared alternately teasing Lisa mercilessly and helping her through the toughest decisions. With a clear vision in mind, we had criteria for deciding what stayed and what was no longer needed. Anything that contributed to their vision for that space stayed. Everything else went.

The sweet spot

Jared, Lisa, and I spent two days clearing the clutter from their home. We went through every room, figuring out what they wanted from each space and whether its contents served that purpose. We made some tough decisions. Lisa threw away piles of Cooper's first crayon drawings, picking her favorite three to frame for his room. Jared donated his unused Rollerblades to make room for his new paper shredder. Jared and Lisa made the hard choices while constantly asking themselves, "Does this item enhance the life we want to live?" By the end, Lisa voluntarily threw away or donated every item of clothing she hadn't worn in the last year. "When I'm through I want extra room in my closet. Just for fresh air." When it was all said and done, Lisa said, "It feels like Christmas!" and Jared had to admit, "It's like I just graduated from school. No tests hanging over my head. Nothing is due. I feel free."

We've all had a taste of that relief and joy. If you've ever played tennis or another racket sport, think about when you hit the ball on the sweet spot. You're laboring to hit the ball, using all your might, but when the point of connection is perfect, everything suddenly feels smooth and easy. Or think of the feeling you have when you've just mailed in your taxes. Or when you totally clear your desk before going on vacation. You can walk out of your office, turn off the light, and just know that everything is in its place, right where it's supposed to be. You're doing your job and doing it well. When you succeed in decluttering it will be because you've made good life choices. And when you're living by those choices, you'll experience the joy, the lightness, and the freedom that come with natural order. That sense of achievement can be yours every day, and I'm going to help you accomplish it, step by step, just like I did with Jared and Lisa.

Jared and Lisa had a million self-help books and endless file boxes and organizing "solutions." What I did for them isn't a quick fix; it's an ongoing process that has changed their lives in almost every way. This book doesn't waste time telling people how to stick pretty labels on color-coded boxes the way so many organizing experts do. For me, it's not first and foremost about "the stuff"—that's way too superficial! It's about changing your *relationship* to your stuff. It's about keeping things that make sense for your life—your real life, not a fantasy of what was or what could be. Stuff is secondary to who you are, and that needs to be reflected in your home and in your life. When you solve the stuff problem, clarity follows. Jared and Lisa did it, and so can you.

In this book we start at the beginning, as I did with Jared and Lisa. I'm going to help you clearly define the life you want to be living. I'll lead you through your house, as I do with all my clients, to help you assess the state of your home without any sugarcoating. What is the room? What's its purpose? What is this item? Does it contribute positively to the life you want? What is the emotion that ties you to this item that stops you from letting it go? What power does this item wield over you? I'll guide you through the process of understanding your priorities and fixing your relationship with your stuff. You'll learn how and why your use of space doesn't match your priorities. That's the first step.

But it doesn't stop there. Once you have confronted the physical and emotional hurdles that cause clutter, we'll work to overcome the feeling that "it's all too much." I'm going to lead you, step-by-step, through the program that helped Jared and Lisa and hundreds of others conquer their clutter. You'll figure out where your problems lie. You'll examine what the clutter is doing to your life. You'll decide what you'd like your home to be like. You'll answer, as a household, a series of essential questions that I pose to all my clients. As a family, you'll decide what purpose each room serves and how it should be filled. Work, play, eating, entertainment, and rest are assigned dedicated, functional spaces that give each of those activities a new clarity. Together we'll break down your house, room by room, cabinet by dresser, and get rid of the extra stuff that is keeping you from living your ideal life. You'll learn to ask yourself, "Do I even remember what's inside these boxes? Do I need it? Do I honor and respect it?" I can't tell you how many people I've met who still have their baby's umbilical cord or the first diaper their child soiled (I kid you not!). Is this the best way to preserve the memory of a child's first days?

Maybe your problem isn't extreme—you're not drowning in clutter, but you've run out of space in your house and want to find ways to bring order and purpose back into your home. That's great! You'll rethink your home organization and discover new space and clarity. And the good news is, the smaller your problem, the less time it will take to solve.

If you're on the other end of the spectrum—a lifelong hoarder—the process will take longer. You'll have to purge, then purge again. If it's taken you ten years or more to accumulate your mess, it's impossible to make it disappear overnight. Letting go is a learning process. You might need to start slowly, and it may take time to discover that not having things makes your life better, not worse.

Ultimately, the job is done. Tabletops are cleared. Closets are skeleton-free. Bookshelves recover from near collapse. From boxes of memorabilia you'll have handpicked the most important, symbolic pieces, given them places of honor in your home, and thrown away, donated, or sold the rest. The dining room table that's been a junk mail storage bin for ten years is reinstated as a family gathering place. The bedroom is no longer overflowing with laundry and toys. It's a peaceful place where love and sleep come easily. And when everything is finally in order, I will show you how to maintain this level of order for a clutter-free lifetime.

A year after I helped Jared and Lisa clean up their home, I got an invitation to a party they were hosting. When I walked through the front door, I saw a home that any family could be proud of. Surfaces were clear. There were no piles anywhere. Even when I peeked into the family room, I saw that Lisa had one desk and the space above it was devoted to her scrapbooking. The rest of the room was a comfortable space that was clearly Cooper's hangout. Every room served a purpose. Everything had its place. Best of all, the house reflected who Jared and Lisa were: a happy, productive, successful family and you could see that on their faces. As Lisa offered me a drink, I said, "Tell me it's this clean every day!" She smiled and admitted, "We knew you were coming. We cleaned up a little. But it only took an hour." As far as I'm concerned, that's success.

I hope and expect this book to generate discussions between you and your partner and family members that are honest and heartfelt. Change will be necessary and it will be a tough process at times. Compromise is essential, but the end result is worth it. When you've finished my program, you will come away with clear priorities and practical new skills for safeguarding them. You will be able to look around your home and see only things that you truly want and need to have in your living space. A home is the beginning of every day. Changing it changes your life.

PART ONE

The Clutter Problem

1

This Is Not
My Beautiful House

THIS BOOK CAME into your hands for a reason. I don't
mean that in a spiritual way. It came into your hands because
you or someone who cares about you believes your life would
improve if you could just free yourself from the overwhelming
amount of stuff in your home. But there's a reason stuff is overwhelming: Everything we own has a memory and an emotion
attached to it. We often associate a person, a specific event, or
memorable moment with the things we own. If you could just
glance at a room and know which things you absolutely need
and what you'll never use again, there wouldn't be a problem,
but it just isn't that easy. Most of the time all you can see when
you look at clutter is one gigantic, insurmountable mess. You
need to retrain your eyes and to reframe how you look at your
things. You need to learn how to see what is in a room and how
to judge its value.

It's All Too Much is a systematic program that I developed
from my years as a clutter expert, from going into hundreds of
homes and seeing firsthand the challenges that we all face in liv-

ing the fast-paced, hectic lives that have become the norm for so many of us. So trust me, this will work. Take a deep breath. Hold on tight. Let's get started.

CLUTTER JUNKIES—IS THIS YOU?

Do you have a clutter problem? How bad is it? Take this quiz to find out.

CLUTTER QUIZ

1. Could you have a party without cleaning up first?
   a. Guests could eat off the floor. Bring 'em in!
   b. Maybe tomorrow. The living room's a mess, but I can hide it away in a few hours.
   c. Um, I don't have parties here. Can we go bowling instead?

2. Do your clothes fit in your closet?
   a. Of course. They're hung in order by color and season.
   b. They fit, I guess, but I have no idea what's on the top shelf.
   c. They fall on my head when I open the door. Is that so wrong?

3. Without looking, do you know where to find your car keys, your unpaid bills, and your home or renter's insurance policy?
   a. Absolutely—want me to get them right now?
   b. All except the insurance—it must be somewhere in my husband's/wife's/partner's office.

c. Sure—just give me ten minutes to find them. Or an hour.

4. What is on your dining room table right now?
   a. Wood polish and a rag—I was just wiping it.
   b. A few piles of bills—and my child's art collection.
   c. So much stuff that I can't see the table.

5. How many magazines are in your house right now?
   a. Three—the current issue of each magazine I get.
   b. Oh, a lot. But I need them for my job.
   c. I have every issue of *National Geographic* ever published. It's an outstanding collection.

6. How many paper and shopping bags are you saving?
   a. A handful—we use them to recycle newspapers.
   b. An overstuffed milk crate plus a few extra. You never know what size bag you'll need.
   c. Every single bag that enters the house.

7. Answer the following questions with a yes or no:
   a. If you had to change a lightbulb, could you find one?
   b. Are all your DVDs and CDs in their sleeves?
   c. Are kids' toys anywhere except in their rooms or designated play areas?
   d. Are there dirty dishes in the sink?
   e. Are dirty clothes anywhere but in the hamper?
   f. Are there out-of-date medications in your medicine chest?
   g. Are all bills paid and papers filed?
   h. Does every item of clothing in your closet fit you now?

HOW CLUTTER FREE ARE YOU?

Score yourself:

Questions 1–6: Give yourself zero points for every A; one point for every B; two points for every C.

Question 7: Give yourself a point if you answered: a) no; b) no; c) yes; d) yes; e) yes; f) yes; g) no; h) no.

Add all your points together.

If you scored:

10–20 points: Uh-oh. Looks like you're a **HARD-CORE HOARDER.** It's amazing that you found a pen to take this quiz. But don't take it too hard or feel overwhelmed: The first step is admitting the problem. We'll take this step-by-step and custom-tailor the program to work for you. Do remember as you read this book that sometimes a first round of de-cluttering isn't enough. A few months after your first purge, you'll look at the same stuff you thought you couldn't throw out and realize you haven't touched it since your cleanup. It takes a while to get used to the idea that if you don't use it, if it's not part of your life, if it doesn't serve your goals, then it's just a waste of space. You'll get there, I promise.

3–9 points: Good news. You're a **CLUTTER VICTIM.** This may not sound like good news, but it means that you, like so many others, have fallen victim to the clutter buildup that's hard to avoid when you have a busy life, diverse interests, disposable income, family memorabilia, and a steady influx of purchases and junk mail. Not to worry. With a reasonable amount of effort you'll be able to get your clutter issues under control and keep them that way.

0–2 points: Congratulations! You're **CLUTTER-FREE.** Give yourself a pat on the back, but don't get lazy. Staying clutter-free takes work. Is there a storage room or an office where your clutter congregates? You can turn directly to that section to attack your problem head-on. And don't miss Step 6: New Rituals. This calendar of monthly routines will help you keep your home spick-and-span.

TAKE A LOOK AROUND

Stuff has a way of creeping into and overtaking our homes. At some point it is almost as though we stop seeing it and our senses shut down. It's there, we have to climb over and around it every day, and yet we are seemingly incapable of dealing with it. Take a look at these common symptoms of overflow. Maybe they sound a little too familiar?

Where have all the flat spaces gone?

Flat spaces are the first battlefield you lose in the war with your stuff. Is it hard to work at your desk because it's covered in papers? How about the coffee table? How long have those magazines been there? Is there enough room on your kitchen counter to prepare food, or is the counter crowded with appliances or cereal boxes or storage canisters? The top of the television is not meant to be used as a shelf, nor are most windowsills. Is your bed covered in clothes? How about the largest flat space in your house—your floor. Has the floor disappeared? If the flat spaces in your house have been lost to clutter, it's time to win them back.

Does everything serve its purpose?

How can you tell when your stuff starts to take over? The big, blinding neon sign is what I like to call "system overload." System overload is when your rooms lose functionality. A kitchen counter that should be used for food preparation becomes a storage shelf. A desk turns into a platform for stacking piles of paper. You have too many dishes for the kitchen so they overflow into the laundry room. My clients Owen and Gina were like this—he stored his medical dictionaries in the guest bathtub. In the worst cases, getting across a room can be an obstacle course. Gina was so busy saving every piece of clothing her son, Michael, ever wore that she completely filled up what could have been a lovely playroom for Michael.

System overload usually happens gradually. It's not like you come downstairs one day and make a decision that you'd rather fill the basement with old lawn furniture and off-season clothes than have a place where the family can gather for movie night. You stop making decisions about how you want to use your space because you're too busy desperately looking for places where the stuff can go. When things are stored in rooms where they don't belong and serve no purpose, you're no longer controlling your stuff. Your stuff is controlling you.

So think about your house. Does each room serve its intended purpose? Is each piece of furniture, countertop, or appliance used to do what it was designed to do? If the answer is no, it's time to rethink your use of each space.

WHAT'S THE COST OF CLUTTER?

Nobody's perfect. My friend Nico always says, "Who wants to be absolutely clean and organized? Where's the fun in that?" There's no need to lead a sterile life and I am definitely the first to argue against that. Life is definitely for living, but your disorganization can cross the line. Let's think about what your clutter is costing you—possibly in ways you've never considered before.

What's it costing you emotionally?

We often hold on to stuff we don't need because we feel emotionally attached to it. I was recently digging my way out of a garage of clutter and found a battered, rusty bike. I asked my client Patti about it. Her eyes lit up and she told me that the bike made her think of her childhood with her brother and how they'd have races around their home. What she saw and what I saw when we looked at the bike were two entirely different things. Our possessions can remind us of a time past or someone we've lost. A set of china is a family heirloom that one's grandmother loved. This bassinet is a souvenir of an age one's kids will never be again. These cheerleader pom-poms are a memento from "the best time" of one's life. But it's time to look at the other emotions that come with living in an overstuffed home. No one should feel stressed out when they open the door to their own home. No one has to. Your home is within your control. It should be the place where you escape all negative forces in the world. Your home should be the antidote to stress, not the cause.

What does your life look like?

Maybe you think your problems aren't that simple, that you can't just clean up your house to make all your troubles disappear. True, decluttering isn't a replacement for psychotherapy. But I'll tell you this: If your home is a mess, if it's out of control, then it's most likely your relationships are feeling the pain. One couple I worked with had been married for five years. Their home was full of furniture that they referred to as "his" or "hers." When they blended their homes, they had both brought a great deal of stuff into the relationship, and they had never figured out what was ideal for "them" and "their" new space. They fought constantly about the clutter. They could barely function in their living space, and yet wondered why their emotional life was in tatters. To me, the solution was obvious: Clearing the clutter in your physical space will go a long way toward clearing the clutter in your mind and your relationships.

HOW DID WE GET HERE?

There's a stuff epidemic in this country. We live in one of the most prosperous nations on earth, and we measure our success by material accumulation. Everywhere we look we are encouraged to buy more. Love your kids? Prove it by giving them the best clothes, games, sports paraphernalia, or the latest video game system. Just got a raise or a better job? Time to show it off with a bigger TV or a flashy new car or more (and expensive) clothes. In two-income families where there's barely time to relax, we try to find happiness by buying more stuff. Everywhere we turn, we're told that more is better. We supersize our food. We buy two for the price of one instead of buying one at half price. But for many, it has become clear that instead of bringing happiness and peace of mind, all this stuff is stressing us out and alienating us from our families, our partners, our dreams. Sure, some stuff does improve your life. Of course it does. Who can argue with a comfortable home and a nice car? But where do you draw the line? Did you know that the size of the average new house in this country has grown almost 50 percent in the last thirty years? And all this while the average family size has declined. With more space has come the urge to fill it with more stuff. Unfortunately, more stuff doesn't guarantee greater happiness. And when happiness doesn't come, you buy more, thinking that's the answer. Instead of bringing you closer to the life you want to live, your stuff starts getting in the way.

Disposable income

What is all this stuff we keep acquiring? A lot of it comes down to discretionary spending—those things we choose to buy with the money we have sitting in our purses, pockets, or wallets. You might be surprised to learn where most Americans spend their disposable income.

In any year, more than two-thirds of households in this country spend a sizable portion of their disposable income on videos and DVDs, music and CDs, books and magazines, specialized personal care products, and candles. More than one-third of households buy collectibles, craft supplies, and sporting goods. Not surprisingly, the way we spend our money breaks down along gender lines. Men buy more technology (videos, TVs) and sporting goods, while women buy more books, magazines, personal care products, and crafting supplies.

There is nothing wrong or bad about these purchases—some of them are educational or entertaining—but how many of them have lasting value? What do you have to show at the end of any one year for the money you have spent? Is it a home equipped with valuable and useful items or just more clutter? No matter how you break it down, there's no getting around the truth of the matter: This is the stuff that causes many people's clutter issues. Stuff we don't need. Stuff we buy for our own pleasure, often on impulse, that has little long-term usefulness and adds little to our long-term quality of life.

The new town square

Who can blame us for all this consumerism? All across the country the mall has become the new town square. We spend our leisure and recreation time at the mall. Walking clubs go to the mall for exercise. You can even have an overnight campout at the Mall of America! As we grow up, for many, the mall brings our first taste of freedom—the first place our parents might send us off on our own, telling us to meet up with them in an hour. This is how we—or our children—come to associate social freedom with a retail environment. No wonder we're drawn back there as adults.

It's not just childhood experiences that draw us to malls. Hands down, shopping is the most accessible form of stimulation. When you're bored and looking for something to do on a Saturday afternoon, shopping is a whole lot easier than planning a picnic. And it's not weather dependent. Plus, there's so much to look at. In the 1950s, a typical corner store stocked one thousand items. Now a Wal-Mart superstore holds about 130,000 items, offering hours of exploration and potential purchasing for the whole family. And retail therapy is no joke. Having new things is exciting and makes you feel like you're changing your life for the better. Your skin will be softer, or you'll have something better to watch on TV, or a new coat will impress your colleagues. Ever left a superstore or a mall without making a single purchase? It's very, very hard to do.

Saying good-bye . . . forever

I've already told you you're not alone. America has a problem with overaccumulation. It's abundantly clear if you spend one minute noticing how many self-storage facilities have sprung up in your neighborhood.

Now what's so bad about renting storage space, you ask? It's a way of not dealing with your clutter. You're saving things you don't need or want by dumping them in a black hole you'll probably never unpack, and you're spending extra money every month to store them.

Think about it from a money standpoint. You're increasing your housing costs without increasing your standard of living. Is it worth it? Think about it from a psychological perspective. You're hiding away stuff you really should deal with, postponing the issue to some undetermined future date. Is that how you deal with all your problems? I sure hope not. Look, if you have a sudden change of situation, okay, I'll definitely cut you some slack. But as soon as you've rented the space for longer than a year, you have to accept that your situation isn't temporary. Your life has actually changed. You need to deal with the change head-on.

Remember that you are beginning a *process* that will help you change the way you see your stuff. I'm here to help you figure out what's truly important and what holds meaning for your life. Let's get started.

2

Excuses, Excuses

WE ACQUIRE THINGS throughout our lives. Some things are given to us, some left to us, some we find, and most we purchase. Everything in your home is there with your permission. All the stuff in your house is there because you think it holds answers, evokes memories, contains a promise, or serves a purpose. You might need those used skis if you ever manage to take another ski trip. You might need those negatives if your kids want copies of the family albums. You might use that china if you have a dinner party for twenty. You will remember the great times at high school if you look through those old yearbooks. You will be a smarter person if you read all the books you have purchased. If all that is true, then why are you reading this book? Is it possible that you were drawn to this book because the stuff you have isn't bringing you closer to the life you want or fulfilling the expectations that you have? Too much stuff can actually create a physical barrier between you and what's really important.

For most of the people I work with, this sense of unease

with the things they own grows over time until it is almost overwhelming. They hate the clutter-filled and disorganized lives
they live and yet are unable to change. They know deep within
themselves that they own too much and yet they continue to buy
things. They can see that their homes are overrun, but still, they
bring more stuff through the front doors without ever removing
anything from their houses. This accumulated stuff wields
amazing power—the power to paralyze and control.

You think you treasure the things you hold on to, but you're
reading this book because you don't like how they've taken over
your life. You say you want to let go, but something stands in
your way. Not only can't you see any of your stuff as disposable,
you also can't bear the idea of getting rid of it. I've heard all the
excuses and I'm pretty sure I've heard yours.

EXCUSE #1: "I MIGHT NEED IT ONE DAY."

Some of us are afraid of the mysteries that the future holds. Life
can take some pretty scary turns. Who knows what could happen? You want to be prepared. You can't throw away that collection of empty shoeboxes. Your daughter might need one for a
school project! You can't get rid of those skinny jeans. You
might lose twenty pounds! Those old, funky clothes might be
good for Halloween or a costume party, not to mention the piles
of ticket stubs for a scrapbook you might find time to make
someday and the broken toys you have every intention of repair-
ing. This is "I might need it one day" clutter.

We all know it's smart to plan ahead. We all have projects
that have to wait for later. And most of us experience changing
bodies and changing fashions that put our clothes into what
might only be temporary storage. It's hard to let go of things
that don't seem to have fulfilled their purpose. You only wore
those jeans once and they were expensive. This lamp works per-

fectly well, it just doesn't look good in this house. It's okay to hold on to one or two items of reasonable size that have a genuine chance of a future life. But let's be honest. Is it really only one or two items? Or are you saving enough stuff to furnish a whole alternate universe in which a skinnier you uses that dusty abdominal crunch machine every morning before inserting all your photos into a new album and then dons that old wig you've been storing for a costume party you're hosting at which everyone will be lounging in the extra chairs that have been languishing in your basement for the last six years?

Clutter stops us from living in the present. The future *is* important. But you have to consider the quality of your life today and strike a balance between the life you are living today and the multitude of possible paths your life may take in the future. We hold on to a lot of our stuff "just in case we might need it one day" and we spend hours preoccupied with this unknown future for which we need to prepare. It's a future that we have no control over and that, for many, is feared. The clutter somehow becomes a life raft for all the "just in cases" we can imagine.

We become so focused on holding on to our clutter that we are unable to be truly present and live our lives fully in the right here and now. Wanting to be prepared for the future is a wonderful thing, but not when it so preoccupies us that we forget that the only time we really have is today. If we are not present in our lives, days pass in which we are barely conscious of what we have and what we can achieve. If our focus is constantly on what might be, we lose the present and the present, like it or not, is the only thing we have.

Most things that you save for the future represent hopes and dreams. But the money, space, and energy you spend trying to create a specific future are wasted. We can't control what tomorrow will bring. Those things we hoard for an imaginary future do little other than limit our possibilities and stunt our growth.

When I urge you to get rid of them, I'm not telling you to discard your hopes and dreams. It's actually quite the opposite. Because if you throw out the stuff that does a rather shabby job of representing your hopes and dreams, you actually create room to make dreams come true.

EXCUSE #2: "IT'S TOO IMPORTANT TO LET GO."

We hold on to our possessions because we believe they're important—to ourselves, to others, to our family, to our dreams, or to our own personal story. We define this importance in lots of different ways.

Sentimental value

Do you hold on to stuff because "it reminds me of the past"? Do you worry that in letting go of an item, you will have to let go of those memories? Has the line between the memory and the object itself become blurred? Are you afraid that if this painting, or this pile of mildewed photos, or this stack of crayon drawings is gone, you will lose that part of your past forever?

Family history

If you're the designated family historian, you're the one in charge of keeping the family legend alive. You don't feel like you have the right to get rid of the "family mementos" because they weren't given to you, they were *entrusted* to you. You are now responsible for what happens to them.

If these items are supposedly so important, the question is: How are you treating them? Are your "family heirlooms" hidden in your cellar? Are they taking up space in your closet? Does the place this "important item" holds in your life truly reflect the value you claim it has? Those who know me, or have seen me in action, know that this is an area in which I am merciless. Don't tell me something is important, has personal value, or is a family heirloom if it's covered in dust, lost in a pile of clutter, or buried somewhere in your garage. If you value an item, you need to show it the honor and respect it deserves. Otherwise, it has no place in your home. No discussion, no negotiation—it goes! Either you value something or you do not. You have room for something or you do not—it's that simple. If we each had a palace, we'd have infinite space in which to cherish and display our prized possessions. Maybe you'd devote a whole room to the porcelain figurines you inherited from your grandmother. But most of us don't live in palaces, far from it. You can't own everything so you have to pick and choose. The value you say an item holds for you must be reflected in the place you give that item in your life, otherwise your words have no meaning and the object is little more than clutter.

Personal achievements

Some of the clutter I see comprises souvenirs from major achievements, often years past: the boxes of college term papers that you labored long hours over, the drawers full of your child's schoolwork that marked his/her intellectual growth, the walls of trophies from your years of high school golf tournaments. While there is definitely a sentimental component to this clutter, it is usually much more about the sustained effort, the hours of practice, the brute strength, or the personal sacrifice that went into reaching a specific goal. Part of you is afraid that if the item is lost, so, too, will the sense of achievement and even the effort that was required so long ago.

Clutter makes us forget what's really important. You're sentimental, you value your family history—these are great things. But at times they come at great cost. I've worked with families who haven't had visitors enter their homes for years because they're so embarrassed by the clutter. In one home, the nine-year-old daughter had never had a single meal at the dining room table because for her entire life, it had never been cleared of the paper clutter that covered it. You think she'd ever had a friend sleep over? Or knew what it was to have pride in her home?

The letters that appear throughout this book are some of the many e-mails and notes I receive almost every day. In some cases I've changed names or stripped away identifying details but the sentiments are genuine and the people who have expressed them are real.

DEAR PETER:
I've never confessed this out loud, but our apartment is so cluttered that we haven't had friends or family over in years. The very notion of letting anyone see what's behind the front door is too embarrassing to imagine. Even worse, I never let our three sons have friends over. Clutter has gotten in the way of our happiness as a family and our ability to socialize. Why do we have all this stuff? It just makes us anxious and angry.

Sarah and Rob are the parents of three beautiful children, the youngest of whom is now five. When I met them, their bedroom was a disaster zone. There were dressers stuffed with outgrown babies' clothes and one whole corner was occupied by a beautiful but now unused bassinet. Rob had tried repeatedly to get Sarah to discard some of the babies' clothes, but she just wasn't able to do so. They didn't intend to have any more kids, so I wondered why they still had the bassinet and other items suited for a newborn. This was a classic situation of the problem not being about "the stuff." I found that the root of the problem was uncovered with one simple question. I asked Sarah if her best memories with her children were in *front* of her or *behind* her. Her eyes welled up with tears; here was a woman afraid that the best times had already passed. She was holding on for dear life to those things that evoked the great memories she had had with her children, a scary thought, for sure. The only way to find out what the present holds is to actually live it; clinging desperately to the past seriously endangers your enjoyment of the present. If you let your sentiment overrun your house, you're inhibiting your family's ability to have a life worth preserving. Ironic, isn't it?

If something is important, give it a place of importance. Find a way to respect and display that memory. If you're not treating it with honor and respect and you can't find a way to do so, then get rid of it.

EXCUSE #3: "I CAN'T GET RID OF IT—IT'S WORTH A LOT OF MONEY."

The hardest clutter to get rid of is that which has the greatest perceived value. I've seen closets hosting a ton of clothes still with their tags attached, garages full of unused tools, brand-new Rollerblades under a bed, kitchen cabinets exploding with still-in-the-box yogurt makers and bread machines. You paid good money for those skis! Sure, you busted your knee and haven't hit the slopes in years, but what if your son wants them one day? What about that broken TV? You've got a new one in the living room, but you never took this one in for repair. You spent good money on this stuff, so you hold out hope that you can eke some value out of it. Holding on to the item feels like holding on to the money you spent—somehow. But these items have lost their usefulness. The TV doesn't work. You never took up Rollerblading. You've been planning to sell that antique chest for years. Now you're throwing good space after bad money.

Clutter robs us of real value. I'm the first to admit that it cost

you good money to buy all the stuff you don't use, but think about what it's now costing you to hold on to it. Think about how much you pay for your house in rent or mortgage. Every square foot of your house is costing you money. So if you have a spare bedroom that is full of clutter and unusable, you're wasting a good portion of your monthly housing expenses on that inaccessible room every single month! Is that room worth the "storage fees" you're paying? Is that a sensible way to use that space?

Think of the other ways in which you are paying for the things you have in your home. It would be relatively easy to calculate how much you spent on what is now clutter filling your home, but maybe there's a more important question: What is that clutter now *costing* you in ways far beyond the initial financial outlay? In stress? In your health? In your relationships with your family members? In embarrassment? Costs come in lots of different currencies.

And don't forget the money that you spend on stuff you never really use. It could have been saved for something life-changing—a vacation, or a child's college tuition. Is the stuff that costs money and fills up your house what makes you happiest, or would you be happier with less stuff and access to that long-gone money?

EXCUSE #4: "MY HOUSE IS TOO SMALL."

There's nothing wrong with hoping to better your circumstances. If all goes well, we do that throughout our lives—get better cars, eat at fancier restaurants, take more exotic vacations, move to better houses in nicer neighborhoods. It's part of the American dream—always planning to upgrade our standard of living.

Clutter steals our space. While you wait to achieve that dream, are you barely able to move about in your home? It's simple math. You can't fit stuff into space that doesn't exist. Yet time and again, I see people trying to achieve this impossibility. Repeat after me: *I only have the space I have.* It comes back to living in the present. You need space to live a happy, fruitful life. If you fill up that space with stuff for "the next house," your present life suffers. Stop claiming your house is too small. The amount of space you have cannot be changed—the amount of stuff you have *can.* Here's your choice: You should either move to a larger place now (and I mean *now*), or get rid of some of your stuff. Hoarding for "someday" is never worth it. If you're really going to be that much richer, you'll be able to afford the stuff you need when you need it.

And one other thought: Just because you have the space doesn't mean you have to fill it with stuff. When I say that you need space to breathe, I want you to clearly understand what I mean. Commit to having open, clutter-free space in your home and you soon discover that the mood you create externally in your home begins to fill you internally. Clarity, perspective, focus, and a sense of openness all come with a clutter-free space.

EXCUSE #5: "I DON'T HAVE THE TIME."

I wish I had ten dollars for every time I've heard this excuse! Life is short—*definitely.* You lead a busy life—*for sure.* Long hours at work—*and getting longer.* Kids to entertain or chauffeur from one activity to the next—*it never ends.* Weekends are precious—*without doubt.* The last thing you want to do is spend your limited free time getting rid of clutter. Come to think of it, you don't *have* any free time to speak of. You'd love to clean up if you just had a day off.

Clutter monopolizes our time. How much time do you spend looking for your keys, or an unpaid bill, or the permission slip for your kid's field trip? Does listening to a favorite CD involve sorting through your disorganized music collection? Does setting up a place for your kids to make Halloween decorations require moving piles and hunting fruitlessly for last year's long-lost supplies? The time you lose because of the clutter is doubled when you consider the time, energy, and effort that are sapped from you mentally and psychologically. One effect of clutter is that you shut down—you have to spend all your energy just coping with the mess, rather than tending to the things that really matter to you. No matter how far behind you are, you can make the time to free yourself from clutter. It's an investment in yourself that will turn things around. And after you've made that investment and changed the order of your home, the time spent will come back to you, with interest.

EXCUSE #6: "I DON'T KNOW HOW IT GOT LIKE THIS."

You're not a big spender. You don't shop a lot. You may not collect anything. You just innocently go about your life, working, eating, sleeping, and socializing. Even so, your home just seems to get more and more cluttered as the years go by. Magazines, books, videos, clothes, gifts—the inflow of daily life. On top of that, maybe you inherited stuff from your parents or your kids went off to college and left the remnants of their youth. It's easy to accumulate things, but hard to let go. Trust me—if you always add and never subtract, you will eventually bury yourself. You need to set limits, and the limits are easy to create. They are determined by the amount of space you have, your priorities and interests, and the agreements you make with other members of your household.

Clutter takes over. One thing that constantly surprises me is

that regardless of the amount of clutter in a home, the home-
owners often express some surprise at it being there—almost as
though someone filled their home with stuff while they were
away on vacation! People freely admit that it is their stuff, but in
the next breath they tell me they are confounded by how it got
that way.

You own your possessions. What you have is yours, or is in
your care. It's your responsibility. It's your doing. When clutter
becomes overwhelming, something shifts in our relationship to
our stuff. For whatever reason, we hand control over to the
things we own. Because of the clutter we cannot have people
into our homes; we cannot find things; we cannot move freely
in our own space and have to compromise because of the con-
straints the disorganization places on us. Don't throw up your
hands and act like this is beyond your control. It won't fix itself.
Step up!

EXCUSE #7: "IT'S NOT A PROBLEM—
MY HUSBAND/WIFE/PARTNER/CHILD JUST THINKS IT IS."

If this is your excuse, you're probably reading this book (or just
this section) because someone's making you do it—maybe even
watching over your shoulder while you do so! You're fine with
the clutter. It doesn't bother you. Your home is "lived in," and
that's how you like it. You'd rather live your life than become a
maid. Your collection may take up a lot of space, but it's worth it.

At a recent event a couple approached me. The wife com-
plained bitterly that the husband kept the original packaging
material and boxes for every single piece of electronic equipment item they had ever purchased. She thought it was ridiculous. He thought it was necessary in case they moved or needed
to return an item. I asked how many boxes he had in their basement. He said it was about sixty. She claimed it was even more.
Then I asked her how many boxes she thought he should have.

She said zero. When I asked him how many he thought was reasonable, he said, "Ten?" The wife resisted at first, but eventually agreed that this was a reasonable compromise. Here's the kicker: I asked them how long they had been fighting about this. The answer? Five years!

Clutter jeopardizes our relationships. People fight about clutter. Frequently when I'm working with couples, one of them will announce vehemently: "You need to tell him/her to get rid of _____." This immediately sparks a harsh response from the other person. As the years pass, these fights escalate and people become inflexible. The argument for who gets to keep what becomes a battlefield, a struggle to get one's way. Once sides are taken, both become entrenched. If one wins, one has to lose. If one is happy, one will be sad. None of this is necessary or healthy. What's more important to you—the stuff you're holding on to or the quality of your relationship with your partner? How do you want to spend your time—arguing about empty boxes or working out a reasonable compromise? With couples, communication is key to solving the clutter problem.

DEAR PETER:

I can't take it anymore. My husband of twenty-three years has buried our house in twenty-three years of crap. I swear, he's never thrown anything away. Ever. If I try to throw anything away I find him outside picking through the trash at 2:00 A.M.! I live in a fire trap and can barely get from room to room. My husband's little "habit" is destroying our marriage.

EXCUSE #8: "IT ISN'T MINE."

How is it that our homes are filled with others' possessions? We borrow garden tools and cribs. We store things for our friends or other family members. Our kids move out but leave everything they don't want or don't have room for in their rooms or in the garage. In more than one case, I've seen someone storing rooms of items that belong to their ex-partner—and in one case the divorce had been more than eight years earlier! You're a very nice person. You would never take the liberty of throwing away someone else's valued possession. But maybe you should.

Other people's clutter robs us of opportunities that should be ours. Think about this distinction. There is a huge difference between the knowledge that you *own* something and the sense that someone has *entrusted* something to you. Being prepared to look after things for someone else is a great and generous gesture, but, once again, it's a question of balance. If your home is bursting at the seams with things that belong to others, there are two obvious questions that you need to ask: If this thing is so important to someone else, why is it sitting in my basement? Whose life am I living here—my own, surrounded with the things I love and cherish, or someone else's, cluttered with the things they cannot or will not remove from my space? This can be a tough call, but your home is just that—*your* home. Don't operate your home as a storage facility for someone else's clutter. Don't let their possessions control you.

EXCUSE #9: "IT'S TOO OVERWHELMING."

I have infinite sympathy for this excuse. You're not arguing that the clutter has a purpose. You're not attached to the past or to a fantasy of the future. You look at the amount of stuff in your life and feel sickened by it. You wish you could change the way things are, but it's too hard. It's completely overwhelming. You're just being honest about your emotional response. I can't sit here and say, "No, you're wrong. It's not overwhelming." All I can do is talk to you about the emotional toll of clutter and hope that you'll see how freeing yourself of it will free you of those anxious, stressed-out feelings. Oh yeah, and then—in the rest of the book—I'm going to help you do it by breaking it down into simple, manageable steps.

Clutter denies us peace of mind. Time and again, the people I deal with attribute much of the conflict in their relationships or the sense of hopelessness in their lives to the clutter itself. Instead of developing and deepening a relationship based on mutual respect, love, shared experiences, and happiness, I constantly see couples whose lives are torn apart from their arguments about disorganization. Many of these people also struggle with anxiety or depression. All of these things are linked—where you live, what you have, and how you feel. You feel overwhelmed, powerless, and paralyzed by the sheer volume of "the stuff" surrounding you. How can you have harmonious relationships or a sense of peace if that's how you feel in your own home? Instead of adding to the peace and balance of your life, your material possessions are causing stress and even physical illness. They're making your emotional life harder than it need be.

> DEAR PETER:
> I have pictures, pictures, and more pictures stacked in wicker baskets waiting for me to organize them. Before my daughter was born I was different. I got things organized and got rid of stuff. I am not the same person, and I do not like it. I am overwhelmed and really frustrated. I have never been at a loss in this situation until now . . .

Clutter erodes our spiritual selves. No matter what your spiritual or religious beliefs are, each of us is called to be the best person we can be. Everyone has a vision for how they want to live and what they want to achieve. We are all filled with potential and dreams not only for ourselves, but also for our children and others we love. All this gets lost when your stuff takes up so much room it becomes an obstacle between you and your goals. The things you own should be tools to achieve your dreams and goals, not hurdles that impede your progress.

Like I said, being overwhelmed by stuff is an emotional hurdle that I can't just snap my fingers and make disappear. But I hope you're starting to see the emotional benefits of conquering your clutter. Those benefits are huge, much bigger than the effort it will take to clean up your life. One of the main reasons I am so adamant about removing clutter is that I see how the space it occupies in people's lives seriously hinders their personal growth and development. It crushes them spiritually. No matter how you look at it, holding on to your clutter is simply not worth it!

EXCUSE #10: "_____."

Okay, there is no excuse number ten, but a list of nine seemed so incomplete. Besides, there are a lot of creative clutterers out there. I figure there's got to be an excuse I haven't heard yet, so grab a pencil and write it in the space above.

Everyone who has clutter in their lives has a way of justifying it to themselves and to others. It's not that unusual. But look around you: Some people manage to find order in the chaos. They're not lazier or richer or less busy or better than you are. You can do this. Some part of you isn't wholly satisfied with your life; otherwise, you wouldn't be reading this book. I'm here to tell you that the rewards of decluttering will far exceed your expectations. You will feel stronger, happier, clearer, and freer. It's time to quit making excuses. It's time to live the life you imagine for yourself. You can do it!

3

Imagine the Life
You Want to Live

WHEN YOU LOOK AROUND your house you may be overwhelmed by "the stuff" that's piled high and wide. The answer
isn't just a matter of "getting organized." I know that sounds
odd coming from me, a guy who is all about organization. But
the way you deal with clutter is not to start with the clutter. Thor-
oughly confused? Read on.

One of the most common errors people make when at-
tempting to declutter and get organized is that they start with
"the stuff." This is a huge mistake. Just moving the stuff
around, into different rooms and new plastic bins, doesn't solve
the problem. In the beginning, remember: Clearing the clutter
isn't about "the stuff." Don't focus on that or you are doomed to
fail before you even begin.

The things you own are a distraction to getting started on
the right path. The key to getting—and staying—organized is to
look beyond the stuff and *imagine the life you could be living*. Put
most simply: It's about how you see your life, before all else. Before the moving and the sorting, before the decision making

and the negotiation, before the tough calls and the tears. I've mentioned it before, and now it's time for you to take it seriously. The first task I give my clients, and the first challenge I want to present to you is: Imagine the life you want to live.

Imagine the life you want to live. I cannot think of a sentence that has had more impact on the lives of the people I have worked with. I'll repeat it again: *Imagine the life you want to live.* Life is never perfect, but we all have unique visions of the lives we wish were ours. When clutter fills your home, not only does it block your space, but it also blocks your vision. It has often seemed to me that people at some stage stop seeing the clutter—even when they can't see over it! They move around it as though it were not there. This first step takes you beyond the clutter, the mess, the lack of organization, to determine how it is you picture your place in the world. It's a deceptively simple question and one that we seldom ask: *What is the life you want?* From this question flows a range of related questions that you need to seriously ponder. In this imagined life, how do you spend your time? How do you feel at home? How do you interact with your family? What do you accomplish in your home? Do you see yourself as high-powered, successful, and on top of things? Do you imagine a rich family life where everyone hangs out together? Do you hope to one day find a perfect balance of work and home, of stimulation and calm?

These are questions that most of us never ask ourselves. We accept what we have and find it hard to imagine things could be otherwise. It is much easier to leave things as they are than it is to take action. Well, this is the day all of that changes! It may take some serious reflection to imagine the life you want to live. Don't just summon up an image of the lives of the rich and famous. Set aside actual time to think about *your* own ideal life— a better life, but one that is within reach. Do this in whatever way you best think through your problems: Find a quiet moment to write ideas down in your journal; use your time at the gym; schedule an hour in your planner to sit in solitude and think; or set aside time in bed before you fall asleep. The details may be slow in coming to your mind. This is not unusual, but it is key to progress, and worth the investment of some quiet time. Think through what it is you want from the one life you have.

YOUR IDEAL HOME

Once you have that picture in your mind, imagine your ideal living space. What does your home look like? What does your living room look like? Your master bedroom? Your relationship? Your career? The backseat of your car? Fix those images in your mind. If it helps, make drawings or jot down notes. Find photos in magazines that match what you imagine. Walk, think, daydream, ponder—do whatever you need to do to make that vision as real as possible.

Once you have an image of what you'd like your life and your home to be, take an actual look around your home. Don't be methodical . . . yet. We're going to start the nitty-gritty of purging possessions in the next chapter. For now I want you to just practice a new way of looking at your stuff and your space. The gulf between what you have and what you want can be enormous, and the emotional response just as tremendous. For many of my clients, this stage of the process can be earth-shattering, as though for the first time in many years blinders have been removed from their eyes. They see how they've been living and what they own in a new light. Like them, if clutter is your issue, then your current life is probably nowhere near where you want it to be. Don't worry—we will get you there!

I worked with a couple, Dylan and Jen, who wanted the master bedroom of their Oakland house to be a sanctuary, a romantic escape from the kids, but it was overrun with toys. The kids had appropriated the TV for video viewing and the armchair was piled high with laundry.

I have a number of questions that help couples focus their attention on the place they would like to be. I know that sometimes these questions can seem razor sharp, but I don't have time to waste, nor do you when it comes to living the life you want. It was time for one of those questions.

I asked Dylan, "If you met Jen for the first time today, is this the bedroom you'd want to bring her home to?" Ask yourself the same question now. Look at your master bedroom and consider the intimate relationship you share with your partner. If your bedroom isn't the romantic ideal for the two of you, why not? It drives me crazy when I see master bedrooms cluttered with dirty clothes, empty food containers, kids' toys, wrapping paper, and even car parts. Remember the key questions: What is the life you want to live? What is your vision for your master bedroom? What is your vision for your romantic relationship? Does this room reflect that vision? The answers are and always will be linked.

I met a woman from Michigan who told me that now that her son, Michael, had his own place, she wanted her house to be "her own" again. Her garage was occupied by Michael's vintage Porsche, which she forbade him to drive because there was no roll bar. Michael's "collectible" toys filled not only his former bedroom, but tall metal racks that lined the hallway of the house. I said, as gently as I could, "Your son's in college now. It's time for him to take responsibility for his stuff!" She burst out laughing, shaking her head at the same time. I didn't see what was so funny until she explained that her son wasn't in college. He was a forty-year-old doctor. Forty! At that moment I thought my head would explode! As far as I'm concerned, this is selfishness of the highest order on the son's part and a complete failure to cut the cord on the mother's part. This is not love; this is stupidity! Each participant bears part of the blame for an intolerable situation. The son deftly avoids his responsibility and the mom, in providing an unquestioning caregiver role, sacrifices her quality of life. As awful as it sounds, Michael is exploiting his mom. In the mother's vision for the life she wanted, there was no Porsche in the garage and certainly no toys cluttering rooms and hallways of the family home. Michael clearly wasn't planning to move his stuff out of the house on his own so his mother had to take action. She had to be clear about her vision for her house, and then she had to enforce that vision for herself and her son. She took action and so can you.

QUESTIONS ABOUT YOUR IDEAL HOME

Does this house look the way I want it to look?

Does this house feel like a home to me?

How do I feel when I come home to this place?

How do I want to feel when I come home to this place?

How do family members feel when they come home to this place?

How do they want to feel when they come home to this place?

How do I feel when I enter this room?

How do I or my family members want to feel when we enter this room?

What is this room's function now?

What is the function I want it to have?

In order to serve its function, what should the room contain in terms of furniture, contents, and open space?

As I said in the last chapter, most of us want to be the best person we can—the happiest, the most successful, the most productive and satisfied, but it's difficult to function at your peak when you're stressed, distracted, and weighed down by clutter. Do you own your stuff or does it own you? Does the clutter affect your emotions and your relationships? Does it affect your ability to socialize or entertain? Does it affect your children? Do they have room to grow up? What example are you setting? Does the clutter affect your psychological and spiritual health? Does it affect your physical health? Does it affect your ability to succeed in your career? If you're struggling with clutter, chances are that your lack of space is suffocating you. It doesn't leave enough air for you to live your life.

Change is hard

Change is not easy, but it is incredibly liberating. The change that I see in people who commit to this first step with enthusiasm and excitement is that, for the first time in their lives, they establish a real home and have some criteria for deciding the true value of what they want around them. No longer is the deciding factor how much something cost, who gave it to you, how long you've had it, what emotion you attach to it, or any of the thousand other excuses that we dream up. The single most important factor in deciding what you should have in your home is now clear: Does this item enhance and advance the vision I have for the life I want or does it impede that vision? This is the *only* question you should ask yourself when looking at the clutter that fills your home.

Every time you look at an item in a room and contemplate whether you should keep it, imagine the life you want to live and ask yourself these basic questions: How does your home serve your notion of the life you wish you had? Do the things you own help you achieve that life or distract from that vision? Is there room in your bedroom for you to sleep peacefully? Does the front hallway welcome you when you arrive home after a tiring day? Can your family gather for meals, fun, or relaxation without the interference of piles of junk? Every item filling your home should move your life vision forward and serve a real function, one that you can explain without making excuses. Remember, "Have nothing in your house that you do not know to be useful, or believe to be beautiful." Do your things meet these standards?

The liberation that comes with the answers to these questions is astounding! Perhaps without realizing it, what you are doing is taking the power out of the things you own and bringing it back to yourself. You own these things—they do not own you! In addition, you have a concrete plan upon which to build. Don't be mistaken, this is not the easiest thing in the world to do. It takes focus and a lot of energy, but I've seen it thousands of times. You have to trust me when I tell you that it will be a life-changing experience.

Where is your home?

This first step of imagining the life you want and then specifying what that vision would look like is perhaps the most important part of the whole decluttering process. It shifts your focus away from the clutter itself and toward something much more fundamental—your dreams and aspirations for the new life for which you yearn. Once you have that first step completed and have a clear vision of how you want your life and home to be, you can safely shift your attention back to your stuff. Now you have some criteria against which to decide what you want to keep and what you can let go.

Not long ago I worked with a family in the Midwest. They had a beautiful home in the suburbs of Chicago that wasn't particularly cluttered, but the garage was completely crammed with household furniture, boxes, antiques, and sporting gear. The house itself, even with two children, showed almost no sign of family life. There were no photos and little in the way of personal items were displayed anywhere and what was there was very generic and nondescript. The family's life was literally boxed and stored in the garage. Because the mother had lost her parents at an early age and had recently nearly lost her only sibling, she craved security. Her boxed-up home reflected that. I had only one question that I wanted to ask the mom: Where is your home? As she pondered the answer, she first looked confused, then perplexed, and then very upset as she answered: "I don't know." The family had lived in the house for more than nine years and the mom didn't know where her home was! That's because it was "safe" under lock and key, boxed in the family garage.

Differing visions

It's very possible that you are not the only one living in your home and that clutter is affecting more people than just you; everything gets more complicated when you bring other people into the equation. Maybe you have a crystal-clear vision for your life and what you need to live it, but so does your roommate or your partner or your spouse or your kids. Our lives intersect and overlap with the people we live with and love, but our ideal lives are never perfectly in sync. It is critical for anyone who shares your home to have an opportunity to define their vision and to speak openly about the life they want and the things they wish to surround themselves with. Talk to the other people who live with you. What is their vision for the ideal home? How do they imagine using the space? What is the intersection of your different visions and lives? How can you make it work for everyone? As the parents, are you setting the tone and totally defining the vision or are you giving equal voice to the children? It may surprise you what this process opens up for you and your family, how it forces you to reevaluate your feelings about what you own and what you perceive as important.

Expect some degree of surprise, confusion, and even conflict in this process. I have frequently found that although people may share a common living space, their individual ideas or visions for that space can vary enormously.

When I first started working with Mark and Julie, their home was overrun with clutter. Most of it was concentrated in their family room: books, video games, DVDs, a ton of Mark's bowling trophies and sports memorabilia, Julie's desk for her home business, and a computer for their two kids to do their homework and school projects. When we sat down and started talking about their visions for the space, they astounded one another. Mark saw the family room primarily as a sports-themed den where he could enjoy his favorite game broadcasts and reminisce about his past athletic successes. Julie saw it as the central family gathering place where the kids could complete homework and have a display space for their academic achievements. Given these two different views, it was no surprise that Julie was constantly annoyed by the dust gathering on Mark's trophies and that Mark was forever hassling the kids to put their projects and schoolwork in their rooms. Different visions— completely different ideas of what belonged in the space and how to use it.

The situation was a little different when it came to Larry and Jason's garage. Larry saw the garage as the primary storage for his main hobby—buying furniture and bric-a-brac at yard sales and reselling it at swap meets. Jason was an avid gardener and your classic home repair guy and he wanted lots of space to do both. Larry had the garage jammed with more than a hundred large plastic tubs that were filled with every imaginable yard sale item and every type of furniture. Jason's tools, paint cans, plumbing parts, and minor home-renovation projects covered the floor where the family cars should have been parked. Not surprisingly, the garage had been a source of contention for a very long time. Now they decided that they would devote half the garage to their new car, and the other half to their projects; they created zones for each hobby and only kept what fit in the allocated space. The rest Larry sold in what he called "the mother of all yard sales." Away it all went, and in came the new car—one of their most expensive possessions. It was not until Larry and Jason coordinated their visions for the garage that they were able to manage the clutter and decide *together* what really belonged in there and what did not.

And so it goes. No one is a mind reader. When visions for a shared space are openly discussed, everyone has an opportunity to voice their views. In this way, criteria can be agreed upon for what is kept and what is let go. It really isn't rocket science! If you thought dealing with your own clutter was exciting, you are in for a real thrill when others come into the mix—and probably up for some revealing surprises!

I hope that you are excited by this process and the possibilities it will open up for you and your family. I have tried it hundreds of times in as many different situations and I can vouch for the transformation that has manifested. What I'm trying to do here is help you to redefine your relationship to your stuff. Stuff alone doesn't make you happy and when it becomes "too much," it separates you from what you want and who you love. "The stuff" can very easily become the major hurdle that traps you in a miserable and unsatisfying life rather than assisting you to live the life you truly want. I have seen it time and again—if you open your space, you open your life to infinite possibilities.

PART TWO

Putting Clutter in Its Place

Kick Start—Tackling the Surface Clutter

I HOPE THAT in reading the first part of this book, you've started to change the way you see the stuff in your life. Maybe you've started to envision the life you want and to think about removing the physical and mental obstacles along the way. This is something that gets me excited and I hope that excitement and enthusiasm is contagious. But now, enough of the theory! It's time to take action and put clutter in its place. We're going to tackle your home one room at a time. In each room we'll make hard decisions about what to keep.

To get the whole household warmed up, I like to start by doing a high-speed, low-level purge, otherwise known as the Kick Start.

QUICK AND DIRTY

I am frequently asked if it's tough making people throw stuff away. This is a question that I find impossible to answer for a few reasons. First, I don't think it's possible for me to *make* people do anything they don't want to do. If you or I are forced to do something, it's unlikely that we will ever feel committed to that decision, so what's the point? I don't coerce people into submission. I want these changes to be permanent and happily accepted, otherwise, within a month, your home will look exactly as it looked when we started! Second, the mind-set you have will greatly affect how we proceed, how you feel, and what, in the end, we achieve. I have never considered what I do helping people "get rid of stuff." Yes, there have been cases where 90 percent of what was in a home has been removed. Don't misunderstand me: I love to see the clutter go and cheer wildly for every square inch of floor space that we clear. But what I am doing is helping people see what it is that they need, love, honor, and really *use* in their homes. Once these items are identified, what is left has no place in the house. So there are two ways you can look at this process. If you look at it as throwing stuff away, it will be a tough undertaking. If, however, you understand that from the clutter and disarray you are going to unearth those things that are most important in your life—like a thrilling archeological dig—then what we are doing is the most positive and exciting thing you have done for yourself in a long time.

Keep this in mind and don't worry about making the hard decisions now. Just because you understand the reason you're holding on to the dingy, tattered pot holders your grandmother crocheted—because you're afraid to let go of her memory— doesn't mean you're ready to stuff them down the trash chute. You need to figure out the best way to honor that memory in the space you have. If you're ready to part with the pot holders, by all means, do! But for now, think of it this way: Most people have two kinds of clutter.

Lazy clutter
Lazy clutter is all the stuff that accumulates out of negligence over time. It's not stuff that you care too much about, so you ig-

nore it: unfiled papers, unopened junk mail, magazines, unwanted gifts, or that freebie cap you brought home from the grocery store but will never wear. In my experience, lazy clutter is little more than trash and one of the few purposes it serves is to accumulate on every flat surface in your home, gathering dust and making your personal spaces look and feel messy.

Stored treasures

Stored treasures are things like your grandmother's hand-crocheted pot holders or your child's first pair of shoes. This is the sentimental clutter that you feel attached to and is hardest to part with.

For our Kick Start, we're not going to make the tough decisions that come with dealing with stored treasures. The first step is to take on the lazy clutter, then later we'll go through your other belongings methodically and logically. You're going to learn how to balance the stuff that you want to own with the space you have for it. When you find this balance, you're going to learn how to keep it. For now, let's stick to the quick-and-dirty purge, getting rid of the superficial stuff that is relatively easy to clear.

F.A.S.T.—NOT JUST AN ACRONYM, IT'S A PLAN OF ACTION!

Whenever the conversation turns to decluttering and getting organized, I am frequently asked for a system or process that will help keep people on track. There are definitely some simple steps that will go a long way to ensuring your success. This is one of them.

Until further notice, don't go out and buy anything. I know this sounds downright un-American, or unrealistic at the very least, but you now know that organization systems aren't the right place to start and the volume of stuff coming into your home contributes to the clutter problem. This will temporarily stem the tide of new things coming into your home while we deal with what you already have.

We are about to have a quick purge of as much of the lazy clutter as possible. The goal is to move quickly. Don't worry if you're not ready to toss your size-two turquoise prom dress (you'll get there, trust me) or the brass cast of the first pair of shoes your kid ever wore (I curse the brass dealer who came up with that collectible). Don't tackle heavy emotional decisions yet. Just do it F.A.S.T.—not only does this mean "as quickly as possible," but it also means following these simple steps. This is about to become your new mantra! The first step is to:

F̲ix a time.

Then concentrate on three types of clutter in your living spaces:

A̲nything not used for twelve months—if it hasn't been used in a year, it's time to go.
S̲omeone else's stuff—if it doesn't belong to you, it's time to go.
T̲rash—unusable items and garbage definitely have to go.

Fix a time
Scheduling a time that suits all those involved is very important. This process is an inclusive one and anyone who is involved in it is far more likely to be committed to a positive outcome and some permanent change. When you put the Kick Start on your calendar, take a vow of abstinence: No shopping until the purge is complete. Obviously you can buy necessities, but don't wander malls or stores wondering if there's anything you might want. No retail therapy and no spontaneous purchases—no bar-

gains, no sales, no "great deals"! You can reward yourself (preferably with something experiential and less "material," like a fancy dinner, a party, or a romantic getaway) when your home is clean and organized. Cleanup is a family affair so get everyone on board by scheduling your Kick Start at a time that works for everyone and make attendance mandatory for the whole family. Everyone's going to benefit, so everyone's got to help.

When it comes to scheduling your Kick Start, you have a choice. You can set aside a Saturday or Sunday (or other day off) for your Kick Start. Or, if that idea is overwhelming, you can do a little every day. My preference is to pick a day and definitely jump right in, but it's your choice.

Anything not used for twelve months

Remember that the objective is to get stuff out of your home, not to move it to another room. When we were making the series *Clean Sweep*, it was not uncommon to take a ton of trash from each of the homes we worked in. A ton! I promise, you will be amazed by the sheer volume of unused and unneeded items in your home. Don't spend time inventing reasons to keep these things. Ask yourself these questions as you encounter each piece of clutter:

Do I use this?
How long has it been since I've used it?
Will I use it again?
Is it worth the space it takes up in my house?

Time moves by very quickly. We buy things expecting to use them a lot and very often they are taken out of the box, given a trial run, and then left to gather dust. Kitchen items are definitely high on my list of items in this category. Bread machines, countertop grills, specialty baking pans, and a million time-saving (but definitely space-taking!), rarely used gizmos fill kitchens across this country. In my experience, close to half of what fills a kitchen has not seen the light of day in the last twelve months.

Face facts: If you haven't used an item in the last year, it is highly unlikely that you really need it or that you are going to ever get enough use from it to justify it cluttering up your home. Take the plunge and get rid of it!

Keep in mind my client Rachel's story. She went shopping with a friend who noticed that she was wearing ratty underwear. Her friend suggested they go to a lingerie store and pick up some nicer options. Then it came out that Rachel didn't have room in her dresser for any new bras. Her underwear drawer was full of expensive La Perla bras that hadn't fit her for two years. She couldn't bring herself to throw them away because they were beautiful—and each bra had cost over a hundred dollars! So for two years she'd been stuck wearing the one, gray bra that fit. If you're tempted to keep something because it was expensive, remember the difference between value and cost. Value is what something is worth. You spent a lot of money on it. To throw it away would mean admitting that the money was wasted. Now you need to think about the cost. What is it costing you to keep this item? How much space? How much energy? What about the peace of mind that comes from having a clean home full of things you use? You once made a decision to purchase this expensive thing that you never use. Now, if you keep it, you'll be throwing good space after bad money.

Someone else's stuff

Please understand something very basic about clutter: The moment it fills what should be your living space, you start to deprive yourself of the space you need to live as you should. It's bad enough when the clutter is your own, but it is totally crazy when that clutter belongs to someone else. Are you a professional storage facility? I didn't think so. Your house should not contain anything that doesn't belong to you. This is a no-brainer. If it's something you borrowed, give it back. If you're never going to give it back because it's been too long and you're embarrassed, admit the truth, get rid of it, and pray for forgiveness. If you've ended a relationship or gotten a divorce and you're storing your ex's belongings, now's the time to let it (and them) go. If your kids have finished school and established their own households, it's time for them to pick up their stuff. If it's not important enough for its owner to come get it, then why are you bothering to keep it for him or her? The same goes for family heirlooms that you keep but don't like or use. This is your life. This is your home. You control your living space. Take it back.

Trash

The trash can is your friend. It is your very hungry friend. Feed it. Keep it full and happy. Take pride in how much you throw away. Make it fun. Compete with your family members to see who tosses the most. Award a prize to the best purger. Give someone else an award for the largest item in the garbage. Remember that you're trying to create space. Matter is conserved. Bigger things take up more room. It's really not that complicated.

Remember the goal: You only want to keep the amount of stuff that makes sense for your space. Will all the books fit on the bookcase? Will all the papers fit in the file cabinets? Will all the dishes fit in the cupboards? Will closets be used to hide away items you never use or to properly store items you use regularly? What is your emotional relationship with this pile of material goods? Are these your prized possessions? Is every single thing in this pile something you need, honor, and respect?

Don't spend too long reflecting. Just make your observations and acknowledge them to yourself and/or to your family.

> DEAR PETER:
> I think I got you in trouble. Today our garbage man knocked on our door to complain. He was annoyed at how much work we were making him do. I guess he had a right to complain, considering I had thrown out about half of our belongings. Boxes of old toys, mismatched dishes, old clothes, and a hideous chair that was my dad's idea of a wedding present.

This is your chance to get rid of those piles of magazines, the junk mail, empty boxes, old newspapers, torn and soiled clothing, never-to-be-read books, outdated catalogs, damaged goods, and the years of trash and garbage that you have just neglected to pick up.

> As you launch your Kick Start, keep F.A.S.T. in your head:
> **F**ix a time—schedule a time and make it happen.
> **A**nything not used for twelve months—out the door!
> **S**omeone else's stuff—return it or get rid of it!
> **T**rash—gone forever!

Ready? Here we go.

ADVANCE PREPARATIONS

Schedule your Kick Start

It's important to set a schedule, agree to it with your family or cohabitants, and stick to it. You can do a weekend purge or you can do a little every day. For the weekend purge, make sure the whole household has the day set aside. Pick a start time and an end time. Nobody takes phone calls, friends don't stop by, and be sure to set a short time for lunch and an afternoon snack (you'll need that energy!). Otherwise, no breaks allowed! For the weekday plan, make it the same thirty-minute time slot every day. Set the kitchen timer and go!

Assemble materials

Make sure you have trash bags on hand—filling them is your primary goal. For the weekend purge, make sandwiches a day in advance, have snacks ready, and plan on ordering pizza for dinner. This is serious stuff—no time for food prep! If you don't have any, buy or borrow a few cheap tarps to use for sorting your stuff. Depending on the size of the job, consider renting a Dumpster that can be delivered to your home and carted away at the end of the Kick Start. Otherwise, enlist the help of neighbors who have space in their trash bins for all the extra detritus you'll be discarding.

Define your target area

Set reasonable goals. For the weekend purge, pick your worst room, for example, the garage or the basement, or you could allocate one problem area to each family member, such as different closets or every person's bedroom. For weekday purges, pick small, manageable areas. Your plan might say: "Monday: living room bookshelf. Tuesday: the piles of paper on the dining room table," etc. Move systematically through your home.

Pick final destinations

There are only three options for each and every item you come across in this, your initial purge.

1. **Keep.** This is the stuff that you want to stay in your home. You use it all the time. It's critical to the life you want to live. Or

(let's be honest) you don't really use it, but can't bear to part with it just now.

2. **Trash.** Remember that every bag you fill is space you've created to live and love your life. Everything you decide to throw away is a victory. Make it a competition to see who can fill more trash bags.

3. **Out the door.** So you've had trouble getting rid of stuff because it's "valuable"? Well, here's your chance to either make a little money or let someone put it to real use. The items that go into the "out the door" zone are items that you are either going to sell—a yard sale, on consignment, or even online— or you are going to donate to a charitable organization. Other items here include things that are being returned to their rightful owners or to someone who has a real use for that item. *Once in this pile, the item never comes back into your home.*

DEAR PETER:

During the last year, my mother and I have made over six hundred dollars at our two yard sales while making our homes better to live in and enjoy. My mother is elderly and on a fixed income. With the proceeds of the first sale, we were able to buy her a new oven since the one in her condo was an old, yucky drop-in. The new stove was basic, but it made the kitchen look great and increased the value of her home. All that for getting rid of things she did not need.

Where you decide to sell your items will very much determine the amount of effort involved. This can be hazardous as I have seen "out the door" items intended for yard selling still sitting in a garage six months later. If you don't have the time or the discipline to sell your stuff, seriously consider donating it and getting a tax break instead. Items that cost you a lot of money can often be sold online. There are now Internet consignment stores all across the country that will take care of this for you. They are well worth the commission they take for handling every aspect of the sale.

In donating, call the charity in advance to find out drop-off times and locations or whether and when the charity will send a van to pick up larger items. If you know in advance that someone else's stuff is going to be part of your purge, then give that person advance warning. Say, "I'm going to be cleaning out my garage on Saturday and I'm going to need you to pick up all your things by 5 P.M. that day. Anything that's still here is going to [insert your favorite charity here]." No more Mr. or Ms. Nice Guy.

Plan where you're going to sort your belongings. If you have the space, put three tarps on the lawn labeled "keep," "trash," or "out the door." If you don't have outdoor space or it's too cold, create defined spaces for each pile by spreading out sheets indoors. Don't have room to spread out the sheets? Create "keep" and "out the door" areas in the middle of the room you're working on and box it up as you go. As soon as you have a full trash bag, it goes immediately outside.

YOU HAVE THE PLAN, NOW DO IT!

Game rules

Start on time. You've got a lot of work ahead of you. Your commitment to this project is your first step toward creating the life you want to have. Don't put off the inevitable for another second!

Don't argue. Have the whole family work together on one area so you can give one another guidance. Listen with respect when you talk about whether to keep something or let it go. Remember, we're saving the hard decisions for later. Now isn't the time to argue about whose what is taking up all the space. You're a team.

You all want to end the day with as much trash as possible and eliminate the superficial clutter. Do what you can to get there.

Don't waste time. Now is not the time to take a trip down memory lane. Don't stop to look through your high school yearbook. Don't read letters or examine photos. Touch each item once; make a decision and move on. Only look at something long enough to decide which pile it belongs in. This is why I often call this the "rapid-fire sort." Don't stop for breaks or phone calls. This is a workday. Be your own tough, focused boss.

Make your piles. Move stuff out of the room and into one of the three piles. As you do, assess your progress. Look at the relative size of the piles. Is *anything* going in the "trash" pile? Wouldn't it be disappointing if you spent a whole day cleaning out the room only to end up with the exact same mess you had in the beginning? The "trash" pile is hungry, very hungry. Feed it. Help it grow. The bigger it is, the less work you'll have to do later.

Don't stop until you're done. The last thing you want is to end the day with a bigger mess than you started, so finish the job. Bag up all the trash and put it in bins. Return all the "keep" items to their previous places. Do your best to replace them neatly, but don't worry about finding new, better, organized places for them yet. We'll get there. Move your "out the door" items to a specific area or drop off donations at your charity of choice, prepare them for pickup, or load them into your car so you can take them first thing in the morning. It is imperative to get these items out of the house as quickly as possible!

Evaluate and congratulate. As you finish the quick purge, you will make discoveries. You may find yourself feeling attached to things you know you shouldn't keep. There may be debates in the household as one family member clings to belongings that another wants to purge. When you have finished your cleanup, take some time to discuss your discoveries. Don't fight about them. Talk them over. Does one of you do more of the purchasing? Is someone else more inclined to hoard and save? What kind, gentle, truthful arguments can you make about why something is taking up more space in your home than it deserves? Is it getting in the way of the life you wish you had? Then you have to find a way to let it go.

YARD SALE PLANNING

Set a date. Do this well in advance. Don't choose a holiday weekend. Pray for good weather.

Decide what to sell. In addition to the things you've collected in your initial purge, right before the yard sale, supply everyone in your family with a box or two that they can fill with additional items that they are ready to sell.

Collect sale items. Sort and box similar items, this will save time later when you are setting up. Store everything neatly in the garage.

Tell your neighbors. Let your neighbors know about the sale—encourage them to have a sale on the same day. The more sellers, the more people you'll attract to the sale.

Tell the world. Yard sales are all about advertising. Put large colorful signs on all major roads. Keep all signs the same color with clear directions, the address, and the time. Use humor to draw the crowds. Take out ads in local papers and put notices in local supermarkets or other places there are community notice boards. Try listing the yard sale online or in free community newspapers also. E-mail friends and family and ask them to do the same.

Attach price tags. Clearly price everything with masking tape and bright markers. Put like things together. Use tables to

continued

make the viewing of merchandise easier. Borrow clothing racks. Have a great layout of goods so that people can easily see everything.

Enlist helpers. Assign your helpers specific tasks like managing the crowd, answering questions, making sales, taking payments, and providing laughter and fun.

Be prepared. Have an extension cord handy so people can check electric items. Have shopping bags or boxes handy to help people collect and carry goods away.

Get some sleep. On the night before the sale, put a sign in front of your house that reads ABSOLUTELY NO EARLY BIRDS or else you'll have people knocking at your door before the sun is up.

Manage the money. Have a lot of small change handy—use a fanny pack to keep the money safe and in one place.

Bargain. The idea of the yard sale is to get rid of everything. Bargain like crazy—offer to add items for an extra fifty cents. Five books for the price of three, four shirts for the price of two—you get the idea. An hour before you are due to finish, slash prices to clear the merchandise!

Get rid of everything. Arrange for a charity to pick up whatever is not sold. Don't take anything back into the house!

Above all: Keep your sense of humor and make the day enjoyable for all. Encourage people to haggle and make a game of it. You'll sell more stuff and have more fun.

Okay, now do it all over again. Have you ever noticed that shampoo bottles always say "wet hair, lather, rinse, repeat"? If you follow those circular instructions, you'll be shampooing your hair until the end of time. Not so with the Kick Start, but you will need to move through your house methodically, getting rid of unnecessary clutter until you've done every room. Only then will you be ready for the hard part—letting go of stuff that feels valuable or important.

This quick purge is just a primer, but it will fill you with excitement and a real sense of what you can achieve. Your house may be tidier, but is it shipshape? I'm pretty confident that the answer is no. You've done a good job clearing away the first level of clutter, but now you're ready to tackle the real issues. Now you're ready to open up your space and unclutter your mind. Welcome aboard!

DEAR PETER:

I have purged about three quarters of my old craft supplies. I have gotten rid of clothes that are out of style or don't fit me or my family. I have corralled all our camping supplies into two containers, not counting the tent. I have gotten rid of all the toys my two sons have grown out of. I have gotten rid of things that I collected just for the sake of collecting but have never actually used. I have gotten rid of over three hundred magazines, with another one hundred fifty or so to still go. I have recycled years of receipts. Gone are the games that are missing pieces, and the school papers telling of some upcoming event long since gone by. Boxed up are all the records from being a PartyLite consultant, and sold are most of the extra PartyLite pieces that I no longer need. Everytime I picked up something intending to keep it, I thought of you advising and guiding people on their path from chaos to peace. I asked myself: When was the last time I used it? Do I need it right now? Can I buy another one cheaply? Is it useable? Does it need repair?

Peter, I have donated about eighty boxes of perfectly sellable items to a local charity, and I have another load of about thirty boxes ready to go.

Hash It Out!

YOU'VE FINISHED THE KICK START. It was hard work, but it was just the beginning. If all I had to say was, "Get out there and throw away your trash," I wouldn't have bothered to write this book. Doing a little cleanup isn't going to change your life. It isn't going to radically alter your relationships. It isn't going to make your home the ideal haven you deserve. But admit it—it felt good. Having even a little more room to move and to think goes a long way. Less truly is more. Now we're going to make it even less. It's time to reimagine your home.

Think about it. We wake up in the same bedroom every morning (most of us, anyway). We bathe and get dressed in the same bathroom. We eat breakfast in the same place. But how and when did you decide how all the components of your life would be organized? When did you decide which drawer would hold your socks, or whether the glasses or plates should go in the cupboard next to the oven, or where to store the holiday decorations? Let me guess. You decided the day you moved in. In the foggy exhaustion that always accompanies a move, you had to put the sports equipment somewhere, so you put it on the top shelf of the downstairs closet. There wasn't room for all the pots and pans in the kitchen, so you put some in the laundry room, where they've acquired such a seemingly permanent layer of dust that you never bother to use them. Sure, not every decision was made on moving day. Maybe you came home from the store with a ton of lightbulbs you bought on sale, and ever since then the linen closet has doubled as bulb central. It was a spontaneous decision, but it works okay.

Yeah, well, working "okay" is not enough anymore. It's time to make your possessions serve your life, instead of vice versa. You want to go to sleep in a bedroom that makes you feel relaxed and comfortable? You want to have dinner in a dining room that can be romantic or alive with family dynamics? You want to work in a home office that makes you feel efficient and on top of things? We're going to take your vision for your life and make it a reality.

COMMUNICATION

The best way to manage the conflicts that arise when you're trying to put together a household plan is to be careful how you communicate with each other. Obviously, being able to talk honestly, openly, and respectively with your mate or family is a critical life skill that you should have, regardless of how you choose to live. But it's worth mentioning here to be mindful of each other during this process because having to toss a lifetime of treasured possessions can be a highly emotional exercise for most people. This is a tough job and you are going to engage in tough conversations, so I want you to get off on the right foot with each other.

Establish a basic premise
The best way to enter a tough discussion is to establish where you stand at the start. For example, a husband and wife might

tell each other, "I love you. I want to be with you. That's what's most important to me." If you take the time to remind each other of this basic premise of your relationship, then the conversation has a starting point of love and understanding. This is not just about the words, it is fundamental to communicating positively with each other during the seismic change you are about to undergo. If each partner knows that the reason for the discussion is to arrive at a place that is best for both of you, then even the toughest decisions can be faced and made together. When the communication is not clear, or one person feels that the conversation is a personal attack, that's when things quickly go off the rails. Before you talk about the clutter, talk about what is important to you both. Discuss what you want the final outcome of this cleanup to be. Agree on ground rules and constantly return to this initial conversation when things get difficult or uncomfortable.

Don't make it personal

As you discuss your hopes and goals for the rooms in your house, make sure you don't start blaming your spouse, partner, roommate, or children for the mess. Remember that almost every household is a merged household of one kind or another. People with different backgrounds and different interests fall in love, or answer roommate ads, or are related to each other. Different people have different interests at different times in their lives. What is important to you may seem trivial to your teenager. You have to find a way to talk about your shared space without fighting or you won't get anywhere. Don't let your stuff be a battlefield for your relationships. Instead of focusing on whose mess it is, think of it as a group problem that you're going to solve together. Don't use words like "yours" and "mine." Talk about the clutter and challenges surrounding it as "ours." Remind the household of the premise you've established. Everyone's opinion is important. Taking the emotion and conflict out of the discussion is fundamental to achieving your shared goals. Yes—they are shared goals, even if one person wants to keep everything and another wants to throw it all out the window. You must start from the larger goals that you share as a household. Everyone has a life to lead in this home. You care about each other and you want everyone to find peace and satisfaction between these walls.

COMMUNICATION QUESTIONS

Here are some questions to help you make decisions about what to keep without starting arguments or passing judgment. The goal is to reframe the discussion away from the item itself to its significance in your lives.

Examples:
1. Instead of "Why don't you put your tools away?" ask "What is it that you want from this space?"
2. Instead of "Why do we have to keep your grandmother's sewing kit?" ask "Why is that important to you? Does it have meaning?"
3. Instead of "There's no room for all of your stuff in there," say "Let's see how we can share this space so that it works for both of us."
4. Instead of "Why do you have to hold on to these ugly sweaters your dad gave you?" ask "What do these sweaters make you think of or remind you of?"
5. Instead of "I don't understand how you can live with all of this junk," ask "How do you feel when you have to spend time in this room?"

ROOM FUNCTION CHART

Now that you've tackled the superficial clutter and cleared a little space in your home, you should be able to see what is really possible. Taking the emotion out of the clutter is important. Without doing this, discussions can quickly slide into chaos—trust me, I've separated enough screaming couples to know! You have the basic ground rules of communication in place, so now is the time to tackle the different rooms in your home.

> **DEAR PETER:**
> I really hope you can help me. For the last five months I have been working hard to get the clutter out of my house. I was really surprised that there was so much stuff in every room. I just couldn't bring myself to let most of it go so I piled everything into the garage and basement. Now guess what? My house looks great, but I can't get into the garage or the basement. But it's all things that I am sure we will use some day. It's all great stuff—it just won't fit in the house. What should I do? Help!!

Room by room

We start by getting agreement on the function of each room. You may think this is obvious—some of them surely are—but you may be surprised to find that everyone in your household doesn't share your vision for how each room functions. We're going to start by looking at how you see the rooms in your home. Create a Room Function Chart and give a copy to each member of your family. Fill them out individually, then meet to compare your results.

At this stage, it is best to simply hear what everyone has to say without dismissing any idea. The more comments, feedback, insight, and discussion, the better! Welcome surprises and be prepared for some interesting points of view.

SAMPLE ROOM FUNCTION CHART

LIVING ROOM

Current function	
Ideal function	
Who uses it?	
Who should use it?	
What should it contain?	
What has to go?	

DINING ROOM

Current function	
Ideal function	
Who uses it?	
Who should use it?	
What should it contain?	
What has to go?	

KITCHEN

Current function	
Ideal function	

Who uses it?	
Who should use it?	
What should it contain?	
What has to go?	

MASTER BEDROOM

Current function	
Ideal function	
Who uses it?	
Who should use it?	
What should it contain?	
What has to go?	

ROOM NAME:

Current function	
Ideal function	
Who uses it?	
Who should use it?	
What should it contain?	
What has to go?	

Complete these questions for each room in the house you are decluttering.

The questions in this chart are simple and straightforward. Use these questions as you go through each room of your home, and have a much broader and more complex discussion with your family. You'll never create space in your home if you don't allow space for everyone in the household to participate in open, productive discussions. The following questions can inspire conversation that helps you find common ground when you fill out the Room Function Chart.

QUESTIONS FOR GENERAL DISCUSSION

1. What do you like most about this room?
2. What stresses you out most about this room?
3. How would you like to feel when you walk into this space?
4. What do you need from this space?
5. What do you wish for your friends coming into this room?
6. What do you wish someone else in the family would fix in this room?
7. What do you admit that you should be fixing?
8. What do you have most trouble achieving or need the most help with?
9. How can you help people most?

When you're all coming to agreement on common goals, start filling out a Room Function Chart that best combines everyone's ideas and comments. The completed chart should look something like this.

SAMPLE COMPLETED ROOM FUNCTION CHART

LIVING ROOM

Current function	Bill paying and storage for Dad's sports memorabilia
Ideal function	Formal entertaining
Who uses it?	Dad
Who should use it?	Mom and Dad, kids on special occasions
What should it contain?	Couch, chairs, and tables free of piles Clear floor space
What has to go?	Sports memorabilia. And we need room in the office so Dad can pay the bills in there.

DINING ROOM

Current function	Mostly a place where the kids play and keep their toys
Ideal function	A place where the family gathers to eat together. It'd also be nice to have dinner parties now and then!
Who uses it?	The kids
Who should use it?	Everyone
What should it contain?	The dining table and chairs, clutter-free, and room to walk around the table
What has to go?	The toys! But where?

KITCHEN	
Current function	*Where we cook and eat*
Ideal function	*The same as above*
Who uses it?	*Everyone*
Who should use it?	*Everyone*
What should it contain?	*Food, dishes, cooking supplies*
What has to go?	*Too many cooking supplies that we don't use It's too hard to cook and keep things clean.*

MASTER BEDROOM	
Current function	*Mom and Dad's bedroom, laundry transition site, and DVD-watching central*
Ideal function	*Peace and quiet! Sleep!*
Who uses it?	*Everyone watches movies together.*
Who should use it?	*It'd be nice to watch the movies in the den and to have a little privacy.*
What should it contain?	*Our bed, our clothes*
What has to go?	*The TV and the DVD collection . . . crazy, but worth a try*

Complete these questions for each room in the house you are decluttering.

If you all agree, great! But don't be surprised if your husband is perfectly content using the dining room as bill payment central, or the kids think the basement should be converted to a digital media control room while you're determined to make it into an office or craft room.

ANTICIPATE CONFLICT

Chances are that everyone has an opinion—even some very strong ones. Here are some of the most common conflicts that will probably crop up during this activity:

Conflicting visions

So you've all written down different ideas for how that over-stuffed, useless guest room could best serve your needs. Now what? Let each family member make a case for his or her vision. Talk about what the family needs most. Is the home office critical to supporting the family? Is the dining room the best place for social gathering? Is there a mother-in-law who makes frequent visits and needs a place to stay? Does a hobby deserve the space it consumes or is it a fantasy that will never come true?

Multipurposes

Often the problem isn't that a family disagrees—it's that the room needs to serve more than one function. The recreation room in the basement is the "only" place to store family heirlooms. The office "has" to double as a guest room. First, consider whether these multiple uses of a space are reasonable or just an excuse. If most of your living areas are being used as storage, then you are not using your space for maximum personal benefit. This kind of excessive storage does not serve a legitimate purpose in your life. On the other hand, having an office that doubles as a guest room is not uncommon or unreasonable. Look for ways to make the room's purposes overlap. Replace a bed with a sleep sofa; use a file cabinet that doubles as a nightstand. Simple solutions can help end confusion or chaos in the room.

As you work through the process of decluttering your home, you must remember that compromise is important. Decisions about shared space need to be made on the basis of what is best for the whole family. This can be difficult, but if the whole family is involved, there is a greater chance of everyone accepting the outcome. And remember—just because you're the parent doesn't mean what you say automatically goes!

IDENTIFY SPECIFIC ZONES WITHIN ROOMS

Rooms are used for different purposes—often at the same time. In order to decide what should stay and where, you need to identify the different activities that take place within each room. For example, in your family room you might watch TV and listen to music (CDs, DVDs, and video games), enjoy reading (books and magazines), and regularly wrap gifts (paper, ribbons, scissors, and possibly a regifting cupboard). In your guest room, along with a bed for visitors, there may also be a desk for paying bills and handling family business, as well as space for some hobby or craft. It's okay to have a room that fulfills multiple functions so long as what's needed for these different activities isn't mixed together.

After you identify what you want do in the room, you must specify zones or areas for each activity. This is a key part of getting a space organized and keeping it that way. Once you begin organizing, these zones become the center for specific items related to the designated activity. In this way it becomes immediately clear where things belong, where to find things, and where to return them. Thinking about rooms in terms of zones or activities both helps you keep clutter at bay and helps you understand how you use your spaces.

SAMPLE ZONES

MASTER BEDROOM
Sleeping
Relaxation
Clothes
Shoes
Off-season clothes and shoes
Reading

KID'S BEDROOM
Sleeping
Clothes
Shoes
Homework
Toys
Reading
Crafts
Music

FAMILY ROOM
Media—music and TV/video/DVD
Reading
Games
Collectibles
Photos

HOME OFFICE
Bill paying
Reading
Studying
Computer work
Mail
Files
Scrapbooking
Crafting

KITCHEN
Preparation
Cooking
Cleanup
Eating
Storage

GARAGE, BASEMENT, AND
    OTHER STORE ROOMS
Garden supplies
Laundry
Tools
Paint and chemicals
Sporting gear
Seasonal decorations
Workbench

BATHROOM
Cleaning supplies
Personal products
Extra products
Shared products
Medicine

LIVING ROOM
Relaxation
Reading
Storage

DINING ROOM
Eating
Storage
Collectibles
Formal china
Entertaining supplies

DO THE MATH

People often seem oddly disappointed when they're working with me and suddenly realize that much of what I do isn't magic, just plain old common sense mixed with a good eye for space. It really makes me smile.

Everything that I do is based on solid principles and a lot of experience. When I walk into a room, I can pretty quickly sum up what will fit where and how best to organize things. This "sense" is the result of experience, but a lot of it is also simple mathematics that you can do without having me in your home. It's simple—you just need to calculate how many items will fit into a given space.

INTRODUCTION TO THE MATH OF "THE STUFF"

You have three eight-foot shelves to hold your VHS tapes, CDs, and DVDs. That's twenty-four linear feet of space.

Approximately eleven VHS tapes or twenty DVD holders take one foot of space.

Approximately twenty-nine CD cases take one foot of space. So, do the math.

If you want one shelf for each, then you can have a total of 88 VHS tapes, 160 DVDs, and 232 CDs.

Here's how you do the math for any space. First, measure your shelving space or hanging space and use the table below to work out how many of any item will fit into that space. Then sort your belongings until you get to a number you know will comfortably fit into the space you have. If you're feeling ambitious, get rid of even more so you'll have room to grow.

STUFF MATH CHEAT SHEET

ITEM	NUMBER THAT WILL FIT INTO ONE FOOT OF SPACE
VHS tapes	11
DVD cases	20
CDs in jewel cases	29
Magazines box with ten magazines	3 (thirty magazines total)
Books	12
Jeans/pants	12
Shirts/blouses	15
Heavy jackets/suits	6
Shoes	Estimate about eight inches per pair.

As you draw up your plan for the rooms, let math be your guide. What's physically possible for the space? Measure the total length of your bookshelves. How much linear footage for books do you actually have? How many books will fit there? What is the hanging space you have available? Assess how many items will hang in that space so you know what to discard. You need to assess your space limitations and design accordingly. This will also help take some of the emotion out of the discussion. You only have the space you have!

> DEAR PETER:
> Yesterday I left Maui, my home for the past thirteen years. I thinned my possessions to less than one hundred cubic feet. Time after time, as I contemplated whether to keep an item or to dispose of it, your words echoed in my brain:
>
> Mementos are not memories. Just because it was a gift does not mean you must keep it forever.
>
> If it is important, then keep it in a condition that shows that it is important.
>
> You have had a profound effect on my life. I thank you from the bottom of my heart. Mahalo nui loa.

HOMELESS STUFF

Once you decide the purpose that a room serves, you'll immediately see that some stuff doesn't belong. If you're making the basement into a family room, then what are you going to do with the boxes of sports gear? There's nowhere else for them to go. That's why they're here in the first place! Aha! This is where you're going to push yourself and start making hard decisions. If it doesn't fit into the everyday purpose of the room and there is nowhere else to suitably store it, is it really worth keeping? Easier said than done, I know. So for now, we'll put that troubling notion aside. What you need to do right now is agree as a household on the Room Function Chart. We'll get to the hard parts later.

THE PLAN

Now take what you've discussed about each room's use and purpose and put together a unified room plan for the entire

house. Stay focused. Remember that rooms serve functions.
Life is lived in the present, not in the future or past. Keep asking
yourself: What is most important to me? How do I want to
spend my time? How will I live in this house? For this to work,
everyone must participate in this process and sign off on the
plan.

Step 3

Conquer Your Home

YOU'VE TAKEN THE FIRST BIG STEPS in conquering your clutter and getting organized. When you did the Kick Start you tackled the superficial stuff—you got rid of everything you knew was trash and everything that you weren't very committed to keeping. Although you only skimmed the surface, you should have noticed a subtle but obvious change to your living space. A little less clutter. A little more open space. Not quite so suffocating. A great start. When you made your Room Function Chart, you agreed as a household how your home can best fulfill your various needs and desires. Now we're going to make that Room Function Chart a reality. How do we do this? Room by room.

WHERE TO BEGIN

Many of the people I work with think that if they just "clean it up," or hide it away in a storage facility, that will solve their clutter problem. Nothing could be further from the truth. Clutter takes years to accumulate so it's impossible to get rid of overnight. And even if you could, that wouldn't solve the problem for long. What we are doing here is not so much a single big event but part of a system or process that will become a part of the daily routine of your life. If you make the organizational principles that you learn here part of your daily life, you will conquer clutter once and for all. It really is a life-changing process!

The Trash Bag Tango

I constantly hear: "I don't know where to start. It all seems so overwhelming." The best way to make the job less overwhelming is to break it down into smaller, manageable parts—to tackle it room by room. Every room has its own challenges. If you look at the room guides that follow and still feel daunted, try easing yourself into it with a version of the Kick Start that I call the Trash Bag Tango. Grab two trash bags. Every day for a week take ten minutes to go around your home and fill one bag with trash—old papers, torn and unusable clothing, out-of-date magazines, anything at all that you'd classify as garbage. Fill the other with items that you want out of your house (remember? The "out the door" items). Maybe you want to give them to a friend or family member or even to a charity. If you want to sell items in a yard sale, or online, grab a third bag and fill it with those items. Just a consistent ten minutes a day is all this technique asks of you. Commit to this and you will see some significant changes.

Do this every day for a week and you'll notice a huge difference.

Do it every day for a month and everyone else will notice a huge difference.

Do it every day for three months and you'll conquer the clutter in your home.

Now take the plunge

The Trash Bag Tango may dance you to the finish line, but most people need a little more guidance. Remember all those excuses we use for keeping stuff? Now we're going to go through your house, room by room, and help you overcome your attachment to items that don't help you live the life you want. You can do these rooms in any order. I suggest you do them from most cluttered to least. And if you start feeling like doing the whole house is all too much, just commit to doing one room at a time. See how it goes. See if it changes. See if *you* change. We'll take it from there.

THE GROUND RULES

For every room you approach, there are three critical steps.

1. Think It Through
   For each room I'll ask you to think about what's particular to that room in terms of the stuff that needs to be in it, the stuff that tends to accumulate in it, and how you're going to approach the task.
2. Set It Up
   The setup is the same for every room. I'll ask you to:
   • Refer to your Room Function Chart and have everyone sign on.
   • Establish zones for the different activities that take place in the room.
   • Figure out what *doesn't* belong in the room.
3. Make It Happen
   This is the action plan that will help you make your vision for the space a reality.

Master Bedroom

NO ROOM IN A HOME should be more important to a couple than their bedroom. Disarray in the master bedroom has more impact on family life, on peace and harmony, on love and respect, and on a relationship than it does in any other room.

Look back at your Room Function Chart. What is your vision for this room? A romantic haven? A peaceful retreat? And what is the reality? Stand in the middle of your master bedroom with your partner and survey the landscape. What do you see? How does it make you feel? Clutter can definitely push the love out of a relationship. If there is clutter and disorganization in this most intimate of spaces, is it any wonder that the passion has diminished in your relationship? As harsh as it sounds, it's tough to make love in a pigsty.

Think of the most romantic place you've ever been. Was it a hotel? A weekend spa? A romp in a grassy field? Okay—no one needs so much information. But I'll bet you anything it was a place free of any clutter and distractions that might have detracted from your loving moments. Follow that same basic concept if you're looking to create peace and calm. What do you want from the space where you sleep, and where you and your partner have your most intimate moments? What is your vision for your relationship? Your bedroom should be a space that reflects this and fosters calm, warmth, and love. Reclaim your space. Only you can make it happen.

THINK IT THROUGH

The master bedroom is *your* space. Get rid of the kids' video games, toys, or clothing. The kids have the rest of the house; the master bedroom should be off-limits to them. Tough? Maybe so, but if you are not going to create a space for you and your partner to enjoy, who is? Focus on what you want from this space and keep that vision clearly in mind as we clear the clutter, organize what should belong in that space, and set the tone for your romantic getaway from the cares and hassles of daily life! This is the fundamental reason for getting organized—to live a richer, fuller, and more rewarding life. Get to it!

SET IT UP

- Refer to your Room Function Chart and have everyone sign on.
- Establish zones for the different activities that take place in the master bedroom.
- Remove what *doesn't* belong in the room.

MAKE IT HAPPEN

A little romance
Consider increasing those aspects of the master bedroom that add to the romance and discarding anything that doesn't enhance the idea of an adult retreat and haven. This may mean

making the room less of a media center and more of a relaxation
zone, less kid central and more adult leisure. I have seen master
bedrooms used as craft rooms, home offices, scrapbooking cen-
ters, and playrooms—none of these is compatible with the focus
and function of a master bedroom. When the purpose of the
room is lost, clutter inevitably follows—do not let this happen to
one of the most important rooms in your home. I promise that
the calm you create in this space will be returned many times
over in your relationship with the person you love the most.

Master Bedroom

DEAR PETER:
My husband and I were in a rut. We have three kids,
three jobs between the two of us, and every night it's all
we can do to weave through the piles of laundry and
toys that form a maze on the way to our bed. We shove
stuff off it and collapse, then start again in the morning. Sometimes it's funny—like when my husband
woke up with an imprint of a Pokemon action figure on
his cheek—but most of the time I feel like his sexless
automaton roommate.

Finally, when his parents offered to take the kids
and give us a weekend alone, I decided we'd tackle our
bedroom. My friends thought I was crazy—that we
should be at a spa relaxing—but I'd had enough. Out
went the toys. Out went the video games, laundry,
garbage bags of clothes that didn't fit in our closet. I put
a sign on the door that said "No Toys Allowed." The
kids are always welcome in our room, but they can't
bring anything with them.

We may have lost one romantic spa weekend, but
we got our bedroom back. And with it . . . well, I'll
spare you the details.

The bedroom furniture and your clothes can stay—all else goes
You heard me: the bedroom furniture and your clothes. That's it. Take a deep breath and stay with me for a moment here.

I was recently talking with a journalist who was writing an article on clutter in the bedroom. We got to talking, as is usually the case, about the personal clutter issues she faces. Apparently she has always been considered "the organized one" and her boyfriend has never been very committed to keeping their home clutter-free. Last weekend she decided to clean out the closet in the master bedroom, get rid of clothes she no longer wore, and reorganize the space. When it was all done, she just stood in there for about ten minutes enjoying the feeling that it gave her. She noticed that when she got dressed for work the next morning she felt calmer and more focused. More amazingly, her boyfriend conceded that he felt the same way. This end result—which went beyond just being able to easily find what they wanted to wear—really surprised both of them.

For this sense of calm and well-being alone, you need to commit to getting your master bedroom in order. If your bedroom has become a storage area, or if it's a place where you wake up in the morning feeling more tired than when you went to bed, then it's time to turn things around. Imagine the room clean and set up to be an area for you to relax and recover from your day. How does what's in the room serve that purpose? What takes away from it? You're going to have to clear out everything that doesn't serve that function. Once you do, will you have room for a comfortable chair or even a small chaise lounge? Is the lighting relaxing enough to set a romantic mood? Do you envision quiet background music playing as you read in a corner chair or before going to sleep? Get rid of anything that does not set the right mood. Make the master bedroom *your* place and commit to keeping it that way!

Where does the rest of it go?

There you have it. The first step to conquering the master bedroom is to get rid of stuff that hinders your ability to relax and doesn't serve the bedroom's relaxing, romantic function. Naturally, it can be tempting to keep things in your bedroom that don't serve its function. Maybe it's the only place in your house where you have room for a desk. It may not be ideal, but it's practical. I respect your realism . . . but no. I have to put my foot down. Put your relationship first. Preserve your sense of peace. Enhance your sleep. Find another place for it. Even if you live in a studio apartment, you must create a separate, sacred space for your bedroom. Put up a screen or a curtain. Use a bookshelf to create a wall if you can't afford to have one built. This is too important to ignore.

WORK THROUGH THE ZONES

The critical zones in most bedrooms are the same: sleeping, relaxing, dressing, and storage for clothes, shoes, accessories, and off-season garb. Now we're going to tackle those zones one by one.

You're not fifteen anymore—make the bed!

Once you've cleared your bedroom of other functions, it's time to focus on enhancing the feelings of calm and space that help you relax and enjoy this room. First things first: the bed. It's a zone in and of itself—the sleeping zone. Remember how your mother used to tell you to make your bed? She was right! Making your bed may seem like a small thing, but the bed anchors the room and sets the tone for the whole space. As with many things that have to do with clutter and organization, you need to create the right mood and set the feel in your bedroom. A well-made bed does this by encouraging order and inspiring calm.

You know how nice it is to walk into a hotel room with fresh sheets and a tightly made bed with hospital corners? Bring that feeling home. At the end of the day, who wants to climb into a rumpled mess? It's always better to climb into a neatly made bed. So make this part of your daily commitment to the sanctity of your bedroom.

The bed is flat, especially when made, and that flatness is tempting. Do not let your nicely made bed be anything other than an invitation to turn in for the night. Your bed is not a storage place. It is not a laundry basket. It is not a toy chest.

CLOTHES

Clothing clutter is probably the single most common problem that I encounter. Paperwork and kids' toys often come a close second, but it's those mounds of T-shirts, racks of dresses, parades of pants, multitudes of shirts, and millions of single socks that keep me entertained the most.

Clothing is inexpensive in this country and we are constantly assailed with the newest look, the latest fashion, and the coolest accessories, plus, we're tempted by endless clothing sales and deals. On top of that, we have different sets of clothes for different seasons. Add it all together and you've got a sure combination for excess. In a bedroom, clothes are always the main problem. Here's how to dramatically reduce the room that clothing consumes and the stress that clothing clutter inevitably brings.

Take stock
You have a limited amount of space in your closets. The number of outfits and the volume of clothing need to be tailored to this space. Again, you have to deal with the simple math. You cannot reasonably hang one hundred dresses in three feet of hanging

space—not that many people haven't tried! Look closely at how much space you have for folded items, for short- and long-length hanging, for underwear and socks, for ties and scarves, for the storage of off-season items. The clothing you are left with at the end of this process must fit reasonably into the space you have. When it comes to clothes, it is seldom an issue of not enough space—there is *never* enough space. The real issue is simply too much stuff, and that's where we need to look for the solution to the clothing clutter.

But it was such a bargain!

Every single time I help organize someone's closet, I find clothing that still has the original sales tags on it, clothing that has never been worn. When I ask about it, the response is always the same: "It was such a bargain, I couldn't pass it up!" A bargain. It's hanging in the closet, unworn. Please explain to me how exactly that is a bargain? If you have unworn clothes that have been in your closet longer than six months, you should either give them to a worthwhile charity or sell them online where they will fetch the best price. Get them out of the closet and clear some space for the things you love and wear.

The 80/20 rule

We wear 20 percent of our clothes 80 percent of the time. Shocking but true! Many of the clothes in your closets are either never worn or worn so seldom that you would barely notice if they disappeared. In my experience, there is no such thing as a closet without some clothing that was bought on an impulse, hardly worn (if at all!), and which now has a fine coating of dust. True? If you recognize yourself here, then you really don't need me to tell you what needs to be done.

You don't need me to convince you, though—let your clothes tell you themselves. One very effective way to identify what should go and what should stay is the Reverse Clothes Hanger trick. Turn all of the clothes hanging in your closet so that the hangers face back to front. For the next six months, if you wear an item of clothing, return it to the closet with the hanger facing the correct way. No cheating. If you try it on but decide not to wear it, make sure you put it back with the hanger turned backward. Be prepared for a shock, because after six months you're going to look at which clothes are on hangers that are still facing in reverse. These are the clothes you have not worn. You should seriously consider getting rid of them all.

Lose the losers, keep the winners

Since clothes can be so cheap, we tend to buy them spontaneously without a lot of thought. You see a bargain or a sale and you "have to have it" because it's such a great deal. The criteria for the clothing you should keep are really clear. You should only have clothes in your closet that:

- you love
- fit you well *now*
- make you feel good when you wear them
- people compliment you on when you wear them.

What is the point of clothing that doesn't suit you or flatter your figure or garner you positive comments? Just because you own them doesn't mean you have to hold on to them or to wear them. Don't dress for the life you have—dress for the life you want! Get rid of the clothing that doesn't match your vision and clear some space to see what you have. Give you and your clothes some room to breathe and you'll feel great when you go to your closet to choose what to wear. Enjoy the positive feedback and compliments from wearing clothes that suit you and that reflect the new, uncluttered, organized you!

Wish clothes

I wish, I wish, I wish. "I wish my butt was smaller!" "I wish I could lose twenty pounds!" "I wish I still had the waist size I had when I played football in college." The fact is that almost everyone I have worked with has had "wish clothes" in their closets. Sometimes it seems like there are acres and acres of wish clothes! Of course I'm sympathetic to these hopes and aspirations, but take it from me, wish clothes exist for only one reason—to *mock* you! Every morning you open your closets and there they are, staring at you and quietly smirking. Well, now is the time to end their reign of mockery and terror. You need to gather up all the clothes that no longer fit you, every item that you look at and think, I wish this or I wish that, load them into your car, and immediately take all of them to a charity. Wish clothes no longer have a place in your home.

I can already hear your objections. "What if I lose weight?" "What happens when I am a size eight again?" "But I paid good money for these!" "But I'm going to start exercising soon!" Listen to me. If you are on a sensible diet and exercise program, it will take time to get back to your ideal size and weight. Be patient with yourself. When you get to that weight—reward yourself. Buy some clothing that you love and that is in style. No one wants to see you in parachute silk sweats from fifteen years ago. If you absolutely must, keep one wish item as a source of motivation. As for the rest—let them go and don't think twice about them.

Keep like things together—color and style

A couple of years ago I was helping a woman tame her closets. When we had sorted all her clothes, we discovered that she had sixteen nearly identical black silk blouses. She had so many clothes in her closet that she simply forgot what she had purchased and so when she saw one more fashion "must-have" on sale—the chic black silk number—she snapped it up. Sixteen times!

It helps a lot to keep similar clothing items together in your closets and drawers. Sweaters on one shelf, T-shirts on the next. Hang your jeans and long pants in one area and your shirts and coats in another. This will help you to easily and quickly see what you have and to efficiently consider your outfit options. No more standing paralyzed in front of your closet with no idea of what to wear.

It may sound extreme, but it can also help to color code your clothing. Don't dismiss this idea too quickly. If you place like items of the same color together, it can be a real surprise to see how many items you purchase that are nearly identical. This is especially true of shirts, T-shirts, and pants. We tend to like a particular style and color of clothing, almost without realizing it. Color coding quickly enables you to see how much duplication you have in your wardrobe and how little you need to purchase of similar items in the future.

T-shirts

There are too many free T-shirts in the world, and the problem with T-shirts is that once they come into your closet, they never seem to leave. Time for that to change. Place all of your T-shirts on your bed. Arrange them into like colors. Chances are you have a lot of T-shirts of the same color—and I'm guessing it's white. Remember that you can only wear one T-shirt at a time! How much space do you have for your T-shirts? How often do you do your laundry? How many do you really need? Start by getting rid of one T-shirt for every three or four that you keep. Or decide on a reasonable number of each color—maybe four of any one color. Cut down the total number of T-shirts using either method. Do the same with your shirts.

And your pants.

And your skirts.

Shoes, shoes, and more shoes

When I help people handle their clutter, the most trouble I ever have is when I try to come between a home owner and his or her shoes! Trust me, people completely lose their minds when you push them to cut down the number of shoes they have in their closets, or under their beds, or in the spare bedroom, or even (as in a couple of cases) stored in ten boxes in the garage! All reason disappears and things get very ugly, very quickly. There are, however, some good strategies for downsizing in the shoe department.

First, bring all of your shoes into an open space. Your bedroom may be best if you have the room; if not, try the family room or somewhere similar. In extreme cases, the backyard will do the trick. Line the shoes up in pairs, with similar shoes together—a line for black shoes, one for gym shoes, one for hiking, and so on. Then quickly go through the lines, discarding those shoes you no longer want or wear. Done? Good. Now go through the whole lineup again, this time discarding unnecessary duplicates. By this I mean multiple pairs of the same kind of shoe—two pairs of running shoes; two pairs of black flip-flops. You get the idea.

When you feel you have done as well as you can, go back into your closet and estimate the number of pairs of shoes that will reasonably fit into the space you have. If you still have too many shoes, try discarding one pair for every five pairs you keep. Continue this process until the shoes you have fit into the space you have. Finally, remember—from now on, to avoid ending up in the same situation, when you buy a pair of shoes, you have to discard a pair of shoes. It's simple—one in, one out.

Socks

I was recently helping Jan and Thomas organize their master bedroom when I came across two large black garbage bags filled with socks in the back of their closet. Jan was immediately embarrassed by my find. It turned out that the bags were full of single socks because it seemed that every time they did their laundry, a sock or two would simply disappear. The two garbage bags were stuffed with five years of orphaned socks!

When I asked Jan why she kept the single socks, she said that she was worried what she'd do if a matching sock ever turned up. As if! I made a deal with Jan that whatever socks she couldn't match there and then we'd throw out. Was it worth keeping those two bags for the pair or two she managed to assemble? I think you know the answer.

Empty your sock drawer onto your bed. Discard any single socks, any that are torn or that are soiled. Fold pairs together and only return to the drawer the number that will reasonably fit. You only have two feet and there are only seven days in a week. Nobody needs a drawer overflowing with socks.

Underwear

Just because it is out of sight doesn't mean it should be unsightly! Get rid of any underwear that is clearly past its use-by date. Spare me the details, just do it! Don't keep bras that don't fit just because they were expensive. Even pantyhose go out of style. Get rid of hose, tights, slips, camisoles, and other undergarments that you never wear.

Your bedroom is the most private room in your house. Sometimes that means it bears the brunt of your clutter. It's tempting to hide your mess behind closed doors, but don't forget that the bedroom is the scene of your most intimate, vulnerable moments. Don't let it be overrun with conflicting functions. It will inevitably take a toll on your psyche and your relationships.

DRESSING

We all have moments when we try on multiple outfits before deciding what to wear. Don't let your discarded outfits accumulate on a chair or dresser. Put them away as soon as you reject them. Better yet, if you've taken something off because it doesn't look good on you, don't bother to hang it up again. Move it straight into your giveaway bag.

When you change after work or before bed, make sure you rehang your clothes or put them in the laundry—nothing should be left on a chair or a dresser or the floor.

Accessories

Accessories are the small extra additions—a scarf, a necklace, a handbag, cuff links—that make a good outfit great. Remember that with accessories a little goes a long way. Handbags, easy to acquire and tough to let go of, are particularly hard to store neatly.

When it comes to handbags, I'm going to give you a choice. If you don't use your handbags, you must pare down the collection to fit the space. And if you have room for a prized handbag collection, you must justify it by emptying your purse every night—the way men empty their back pockets—to keep your purse contents spare and easily transferable.

Jewelry may seem so small that it can't possibly cause clutter, but jewelry is very hard to store neatly and most people only wear a fraction of what they have. I want you to enjoy what you have to the fullest through organization, even when it comes to the smallest details.

Start by throwing away all the little boxes that your jewelry came in. They may seem fancy with their velvet cases, but they aren't. Now get rid of everything you don't wear, no matter how valuable it seems. (If it's so valuable, it's an easy eBay sale—easy to box and cheap to ship.) Have one jewelry box that fits your whole collection and separates necklaces, rings, bracelets, and earrings. Try pinning pierced earrings through a piece of fabric so it is easy to see all your options at once. This also prevents them from getting lost or separated.

Invest in a hamper

It's a simple rule: Clean clothes are either hung or folded in your closet or drawers, dirty clothes live in a hamper before their trip to the washing machine or dry cleaner. I have never been able to understand the urge to cover a bedroom floor with yesterday's socks, underwear, T-shirt, and jeans. Consider what you want from your bedroom and then ask yourself if dirty clothes on the floor are part of that plan. I didn't think so. Get into the habit of placing clothes that are in need of washing into a hamper as soon as you take them off. This keeps your bedroom clear of clothing clutter, avoids an eyesore no one wants, and keeps all your laundry in one place and ready to be washed.

STORAGE

The majority of your closet should be filled with clothes you wear frequently and that make you feel good. Use the season switch to review your wardrobe and get rid of the past season's clothes that you didn't end up wearing and the upcoming season's clothes that don't look appealing when you pull them out of storage. Clean and store off-season items so they are easier to find in your closet.

What's under the bed?

Look under the bed in your master bedroom. Traditional feng shui teaches that it is extremely bad for energy flow to have anything under the bed. I don't know much about feng shui, but I do know that cluttered space is wasted space.

Drag everything that's under the bed out to the middle of the room. It turns out there are monsters under most beds—in the form of dust mites. Keeping all this stuff under your bed is not healthy and it's not necessary. Decide if you need anything that was stored under the bed. If you really do and there's nowhere else to store it, put the items in clear containers with lockable lids. Shut the lids tight—and put the containers back under your bed. In six months (or through a change of season if you store clothes there), if you haven't needed or visited what's under your bed, I'd seriously consider throwing everything away. Bag up the rest and throw it in the trash.

Out of sight is not out of mind. If you want your master bedroom to be a sanctuary and a haven for you and your partner, then you have to make sure that includes even the areas that you can't see.

REALITY CHECK—GIVING TO CHARITIES

Goodwill receives a billion pounds of clothing every year. Ultimately, they use less than half of the clothing they get. Clothing is cheap, and the cost of sorting, cleaning, storing, and transporting the clothes is higher than their value. If you wouldn't give an article to a family member, it's probably not good enough for charity. Sure, it's great to get the tax deduction and it makes you feel like you didn't waste money buying the clothes, but if you're truly charitable, be sensitive to the needs of the organization. Charities aren't dumping grounds for your trash. Talk to your local charities or visit www.charitynavigator.org. Find out what they can most use. Although giving to charities is a great way to get stuff out of your house, it's far better not to *let* stuff into your house.

Room 2

Kids' Rooms

KIDS LEARN SO MUCH MORE from what they see than from what they hear. Why else would parents say, "Everything I tell that kid goes in one ear and out the other!"? It's frustrating for me to listen to parents complaining that their kids won't clear the clutter in their rooms, or take care of their things. Inevitably, I've just heard those same parents bellyaching about the clutter that fills their homes. Don't complain that your child won't tidy his room when your closet is spewing clothes into your bedroom, or the garage is so full of clutter that you don't remember the last time you parked your car in there. Model the behavior you want from your children and then I'll throw a little sympathy your way.

THINK IT THROUGH

How a household operates greatly affects what is in it, and the typical American household operates nothing like it did even twenty years ago. The most recent research indicates that many families don't spend much time together. When they do, the time tends to be spent going to and from classes, lessons, or sporting events, or, as is most usually the case, the whole family goes shopping.

Kids have more access than ever to vast amounts of information and a great deal of media influence and advertising. More than ever, it is imperative for parents to be parents, to demonstrate by their words and actions what they value, and to model the behavior they desire for their kids. In my experience, the less clutter and more organization you can build into your home, the less stress, more fun, and greater harmony you'll enjoy.

SET IT UP

- Refer to your Room Function Chart and have everyone sign on.
- Establish zones for the different activities that take place in the kids' bedrooms.
- Remove what *doesn't* belong in the rooms.

MAKE IT HAPPEN

Establish the zones

When you establish the zones with your child, it's important to help him or her understand where things belong in the room and in the house by creating clear zones for like items. This reinforces the concept of everything having a proper place. It also makes it easier for children to tidy the room and helps them take responsibility for order in their own space.

As a starting point, think of the things your child likes to do—play with toys, read, play games, draw or paint, build models, display bug collections, or play an instrument. Create a place for each of these activities. A bookshelf for reading materials, a low shelf to store games, bins for toys, a table for painting or craft activities, a music stand and storage bins for sheet music, and so on. Once you've established the activity zones, be creative in labeling these areas. Get your child involved. Ensure that the shelving and storage units are at the right height for the child and consistently reinforce the correct place for storing and displaying your child's belongings.

ZONE GAME

Make zoning fun for kids by asking them to pick out an item that represents each of the different activities they do in their bedrooms. "You make art? What can you find that you use to make art?" After a while you'll have a pile representing each of the activities: a paintbrush for art, a pillow for sleep, a book for reading, etc. Now ask your child to make signs (or take pictures) showing each of the items. Use these signs to label the different zones.

One giant toy chest

Mapping out zones is just the beginning. Now let's look at the stuff that occupies those zones. For many of the families I work with, excess is the norm. If one toy is good, then it follows that fifty toys must be great! If a child enjoys one game, then naturally twenty games will bring twenty times the enjoyment— right? Wrong. Many parents lavish their children with toys and other gifts to the point that I have found homes that are completely overrun with toys, stuffed animals, electronics, bikes, and a thousand other playthings. Birthday parties and holiday gifts only make it worse. Often grandparents overindulge the

kids, and many parents tell me they don't know how to say no.
For everyone's sake, it's time you learned!

Whether the problem is in your child's bedroom, his play-room, or her takeover of the family's living space, one challenge is always constant: toy management. Sure, we all know toys are important. They inspire, educate, and entertain your kids. But if you manage toys well, you will teach your child so much more than how to play.

Every important lesson that kids need to learn about life they can learn from their toy bins—if only their parents can be brave enough and loving enough to see that for children less is more. (Needless to say, there are a lot of adults who could also learn a thing or two here.) Children need the basics to survive and thrive—love, food, and shelter. Without these necessities, life would be impossible. But they also need two other basics—limits and routines. Kids thrive on limits and relish routines. Create a life model by setting and enforcing reasonable limits and establishing clear routines.

Toy limits

Kids today—their attention spans are so short. You have so much to do. It's easy to give them a constant supply of new toys to keep them occupied. Often it's easier to fulfill their requests (or demands!) for new entertainment than to plan a play date or find time to go to a museum or park. But if a child only has to ask—or scream—and know that another plaything will be forthcoming, how does he or she learn that you cannot own everything? The behavior that says it's all right to acquire and acquire and acquire is learned at a very early age and is a lesson that is very difficult to later unlearn. Isn't that why you are read-ing this book?

The child's first three years set the tone for the rest of his or her life. From the beginning you, as the parent, must provide some limit to how much your child can own. Here is a simple strategy to help you. Provide your child with a couple of bins for toys—two or three—whatever is reasonable for the space you have. These bins are where the toys live. Not on the furniture in the family room, or in Mom and Dad's room, or in the backseat of the car. When the bins are full, that's it. No more toys. Before a new toy can be added, a toy of similar size has to be removed and given away to charity or someone who will value and use it.

> **LESSONS LEARNED FROM TOY LIMITS**
>
> Setting limits teaches the child:
>
> - you can't own everything.
> - there is joy and satisfaction in giving to others who are less fortunate.
> - Mom and Dad (or the grandparents) are not a bottomless pit of supply.
> - you must make decisions surrounding the things you own.
> - you must decide what is important to you, value it, and look after it.

This may seem harsh, but children really do not need an endless supply of things to be happy. And it is a parent's obligation to help the child create a world in which solid values come before the acquisition of the latest video game or newest gadget. This investment when the child is young will yield huge dividends later on in life.

Outgrown toys

Kids outgrow everything quickly, including their interest in toys. It's important to regularly sort toys with your kids, to discard and pass on everything that they have outgrown, that they no longer play with, or that is damaged. Don't do this on your own. Involve the kids in deciding what should stay and what should go.

Arrange the toys in distinct piles—either by type of toy, by age appropriateness, or by length of time the child has had the toy. This will help your children see the toys as distinct groups and make the task more manageable. Agree on the volume of toys that is reasonable to keep, factoring in the size of the space, then work together to that goal.

Be patient—learning to part with the things that have memories can be tough. Don't we all know it! It always helps to schedule this purge right before a birthday or the holidays when kids are looking forward to some new toys.

Toy routines

Just as limits are important in helping kids manage clutter, so are simple routines. In addition to owning a reasonable, manageable quantity of toys, children need to learn the regular rhythm of picking up after themselves. At the end of the play session or at the end of the day, the toys need to be returned to their bins. If this seems unreasonable, go back to the vision you have for the life you want. If you want a lifetime of picking up after your children, this is where it starts. Your choice!

LESSONS LEARNED FROM TOY ROUTINES

This daily activity of returning toys to their homes teaches the child:

- the importance of personal responsibility.
- the fundamentals of being organized.
- the concepts of timetables and scheduling.
- to participate as a member of a larger family.
- to help with simple chores that grow as the child matures.

Not surprisingly, most of the clutter problems I deal with involve adults who have no concept of limits or routines for themselves, much less their kids. Who can blame them? As children, they never learned these concepts from their own parents.

Outgrown gear and clothes

It doesn't just take a village to raise a child. Apparently—in the United States at least—it takes a few major retailers, a number of where-to shopping guides, a detailed list of the latest accessories, any number of weekly sales, a barrage of television and radio commercials, and must-have designer clothing—all of which add up to a whole lot of gear. Added to the toy clutter are the early childhood necessities like cribs, strollers, car seats, swings, slings, high chairs, and so on. "They grow up so fast" doesn't just mean we should treasure the moments with our kids. It also means that last year's winter coat won't fit this year and the high chair that was so helpful last year is now taking up much-needed space. When you combine that rapid growth with fashions that come and go, you have a recipe for a ton of stuff coming into your home but not necessarily anything going out. You absolutely must create a system to deal with the constant influx of clothing and kid-related paraphernalia.

As I hope you're starting to realize by now, the only answer to managing inflow is to create an equal volume of outflow. Don't hold on to stuff just because it's cute or expensive or sentimental. Find a friend or a charity to bring a load of outgrown hand-me-downs to every six months. Talk with other parents in your child's playgroup or school—look for creative ways to pass hand-me-downs to others who will value and use them. You'll make some lucky kid very happy and save some parent's budget serious strain!

INTRODUCING YOUR CHILD TO GIVING

If letting go of once prized possessions is new and hard for your child, try the following techniques.

- *Meet the charity.* Put a face to the recipient of your child's toys. Before giving anything away, go to a shelter or charity and show your child how his hand-me-downs will be used by someone who needs them more.
- *Demonstrate by example.* Before asking your children to donate, involve them in your own donation project. Let them help you find clothes you never wear. Show them how happy you are about finding a "good home" for things you once loved. Ask them if they'd like to give it a try.
- *Situational education.* When certain catastrophes, large and small, happen in the world and in your life, seize the moment to teach your child about giving. For example, a TV interview with a hurricane victim is a way to give a face to the clothes you're sending away. Or passing a homeless person on the street is a chance to explain that some people have a harder life, and we can help them.
- *Birthday giving.* A child's birthday is a great time to pair the influx of gifts with some giving. Duplicate presents are easy to give away and doing it helps get the child used to the idea. It's also a good time to purge old toys and clothes: "Now that you're such a big girl, let's see what you've outgrown."

ART AND SCHOOLWORK—TO KEEP OR NOT TO KEEP

I was recently speaking to a large group of people about clutter and organization. One of the men in the audience had twenty-four-year-old twin boys who were in college. Much to his wife's discomfort, he had kept every single piece of schoolwork the boys had done since preschool. Every test, every homework assignment, every project, every notebook. *Every single piece!* Once it had filled their basement to capacity, it crept upstairs and was now stored throughout the house. When I asked why he felt compelled to keep every single item his sons had ever created, the man said it was because they wanted to go through it one day. Much to his horror, I borrowed his cell phone and called one of the boys then and there. When I recounted his father's reasoning, the boy said, "Let me tell you something about my dad . . . I love him, but he is crazy!" Even Dad couldn't help laughing at that spontaneous but pretty accurate assessment!

When it comes to children's art and schoolwork, it gets hard to tell whether the parents are saving it for the child or for themselves. I have heard all the excuses: "I don't have any of my own schoolwork to look back at," or "She will want it one day," or "It's so good I couldn't throw it away," or "He would be upset if I didn't keep it." Don't use your children as a shield for the real reason you will not let go of your kid's art or schoolwork. It's time to face reality. While it makes sense to keep some of the best pieces of your child's work, is it possible that the stuff you are keeping represents something you yourself miss and yearn for? Or is it that you cannot separate the memory of your child's achievement from the piece itself? Both of these possibilities have some legitimacy, within reason. Ultimately, it doesn't matter if it's for you or for your child because one thing is certain— you cannot and should not keep everything!

Art

Adrienne is an amazing artist. She also is an avid reader, loves collecting and pressing wildflowers, writes magical stories, and finds it close to impossible to let go of any of the art pieces she makes, paints, or draws. Adrienne is only six years old and already her room is overflowing with bins and boxes of her things. In talking with Adrienne, it's easy to see that she is immensely proud of what she creates and collects. She is also afraid of losing it. By organizing her space, placing frames on the walls in which she can display her artwork and easily change it out, putting up shelves to display her collections, and helping her set up a "lending library" for her stories, Adrienne learned the pleasure of setting limits and holding on to only the best things that fit in the space we created. Getting there was a challenge for Adrienne, but when it was all said and done, she admitted feeling proud of the work on the walls and being happy to have more space to create. Having her premiere pieces framed or on display literally brought them into the light and honoring them diminished Adrienne's fear of loss.

There's no such thing as artist's block in preschool, or kindergarten, or even elementary school, for that matter. Say your child paints at least one masterpiece a day. At three hundred works in a year, your child is more prolific than Picasso. I'm not heartless, but we both know you can't keep every single scribble. How do you pick and choose? And how do you break it to your child that a portion of the work you oohed and aahed over should be thrown away?

The answer is to make it a ceremony, not a purge. File flat art in a portfolio. At the end of each semester, tell your child it's time to pick the best of the best. Go through the art and pick one piece to frame and three or four to keep for posterity. The rest can be photographed and discarded. Use frames that allow you to easily swap in a new masterpiece from your prodigy to replace an old one. This strategy enables you to keep art pieces that your child values and loves. It also gives your child practice in discerning what to keep and what to let go—a valuable lesson for life and a real stumbling block for many people who struggle with clutter.

Three-dimensional art is trickier. What to do with the mock volcanoes and amorphous clay paperweights? Again, let them linger for a while, until the thrill has worn off, then decide whether something is for display or whether it was a "learning experience." If you or your child really want to hold on to the piece, make sure that it is displayed well in a way that protects it from dust and damage.

Schoolwork

By now you should have the hang of this! As with art, you must set a limit. Who are you keeping the schoolwork for—you, or your child? Designate a drawer, a folio, or a bin for the work you are going to keep. The size of this container sets the limit for how much you can save. Once the drawer is full, a piece has to be discarded before anything new can be added. One in, one out—it's a simple but effective strategy.

REALITY CHECK—GRANDPARENTS AND TOYS

When grandparents visit they often want to achieve the Santa Claus effect. They come loaded with toys in hopes of spoiling and delighting their beloved grandchildren. It's tough to say no, but here are some suggestions you can give them for more practical gift giving.

- Set up a college fund to which they can contribute.
- Set up a travel fund that, when your child turns sixteen, will pay for her to take a trip with her grandparents.

- Suggest specific toys that you would have bought your child anyway—toys that serve a real function in the child's development.
- Suggest ways they can show their love through *experiences* instead of stuff. Remind them that sharing an experience with her grandparents is as exciting to your daughter as receiving stuff. She won't remember her Elmo doll for long, but if she learns to appreciate new experiences, they'll be helping to create a pattern that will last the child's whole life.
- Take the kids to a show. Introduce them to musicals, ballet, or other live theater.
- Ask them to bring ingredients for a favorite family recipe and to cook with the child.

When it comes to keeping your children's belongings in order, stick to limits and routines. These simple strategies will help you and your children see the value in what is kept. They will help you teach your children to be more serious about the value of what they have and how important it is. You can't keep everything, but what you do keep will be important and valuable mementos that you and they will treasure.

Room 3

Family and Living Rooms

I PUT THESE TWO ROOMS together because formal living rooms tend to be clutter-free—and if they aren't, it's because they're functioning as family rooms.

Ah, the family room. It's everything—a place to watch TV, play games, do homework, pay bills, read magazines, hang out, and entertain. There is no room in the house where people's ideas and visions for the space intersect as much as they do in the family room. The problem is that in being everything to everyone, this room can very easily end up with no focus at all. Instead, it becomes the center of clutter and disorganization for everyone in the family.

By talking through what family members want and expect from this space, you can give specific purpose to the all-purpose-room and in doing so redefine your family and how it uses common space.

THINK IT THROUGH

The family room is just that—a room to be shared and enjoyed by the whole family, so make sure that you reach a consensus re-

garding what will work in the space that you have. More important, don't overload this room with too many functions. Space
permitting, the room can serve a reasonable number of purposes well, but if you expect too much, you run the risk of it becoming the catch-all room for the whole family—in other
words, clutter central!

SET IT UP

- Refer to your Room Function Chart and have everyone
  sign on.
- Establish zones for the different activities that take place
  in the family room.
- Remove what *doesn't* belong in the room.

MAKE IT HAPPEN

Establish the Zones

Gary and Marie have three young children. They live in an 1,800-
square-foot home. When I first saw their living room it was a
catch-all for anything you can imagine—clothing, books, mail,
the kids' toys, crafting materials, even two large stacks of romance novels that Marie had recently collected from her grandmother's home. Once something came into that room it never
left. When Marie was eight, her parents moved across the country and had not permitted Marie and her brothers and sisters to
bring most of their toys and personal items. The trauma of this
childhood event was the main force making it difficult for her to
let go of anything that came into the house. She didn't want her
children to have the same sense of loss. But what Marie had to
face was that her extreme reaction had its own effect on her
kids. Chaos and clutter is never the right answer to trauma and
loss. Only when Marie confronted the habits she was instilling
in her own children was she able to start letting go of the clutter.

The greatest temptation with a family room or living room is to fill it to the brim! This is unfortunate because of all rooms in the house, this is usually the one where everyone hangs out and relaxes. There's no getting around it: Watching TV or movies or playing video games is a major pastime and the family room is where this usually takes place.

Resist the temptation to overload this room. Remember that the point is to hang out and entertain yourselves. The whole family has a stake in this room. Talk about what you each find entertaining. What do you really use to have fun and relax in the space? Once you've all defined your ideas of entertainment, identify what's left. What remains in the room that no one ever plays with, watches, listens to, or uses? That's what has to go.

Keep like things together in their specific zones. All DVDs and CDs should be close to the entertainment unit. Magazines belong in a magazine rack next to your favorite chair. Electronic equipment goes in one single cabinet or shelving unit. Board games go in storage bins next to or under the coffee table where you most often play them.

If you don't use an item regularly in this room, discard it. This room is for *living*. Too much stuff here will only create a sense of being overwhelmed and uncomfortable.

Double functions

As with the master bedroom, sometimes the family room tries to serve secondary purposes. It's not just a hang-out room, it's often also an office or a guest bedroom. I don't permit double functions in the sacred master bedroom (it would be particularly awkward if it doubled as a guest room!), but here it can really make sense. *If* you follow one simple rule: The extra function is a zone. It must be restricted to a confined space. No overflow allowed.

Entertainment

Because most family rooms are primarily used for watching television and relaxing, videos, DVDs, CDs, video game consoles, gaming cartridges, and books tend to take up a huge amount of the space.

Ensure that all media have a clearly defined area. Arrange your DVDs into specific categories or genres so that any movie is easy to find and, more important, easy to put away again. Clearly label the shelves or storage unit you choose so that everyone knows where the DVDs belong. Go through your DVDs and get rid of the ones you'll never watch again. You may be surprised to find that your taste has changed. And when it comes to kids' videos, purge even more frequently. There's no need to hang on to those *Sesame Street* tapes now that your child is ten years old.

You will also be surprised at how accessible your collection of music or movies is when it's organized. The fact that you can easily and quickly locate a specific title will mean that you are more likely to use what you have and not be frustrated by trying to locate something you know you have, but just can't find.

The Ratio Rule

If you have a difficult time knowing where to start, try using the ratio rule to clear excess movies. For every four or five videos or DVDs you keep, remove one from your collection. Give them away to charity, or if you have a friend or family member who would enjoy a particular movie, give it to them, but be sure to set a deadline for all giveaways. At the end of this sort-and-purge, if all your movies still do not fit on your shelves, do the same thing again. Try to lower the ratio to three to one or, if you are really brave, two to one. Challenge other family members to match or exceed the number of titles you're getting rid of. Repeat the process until all your movies fit nicely on your shelves, with some spare room for new acquisitions.

In the future, it's important to keep your collection to the space you have. When you buy a movie, you need to remove one from your collection. Consider having a "most popular" or "new purchases" box that contains ten or so DVDs at any one time that are watched the most. This saves time and effort locating movies and then restocking them. If you keep ten movies there, don't buy another until you've watched and reshelved at least one of those. This same tactic works for other media. Demonstrate your love of movies, books, or music CDs by treating them with the love and respect they warrant and creating a space to enjoy them properly.

Go digital

Take the time to arrange all of your CDs. Choose a system that works for you—alphabetical, by genre, or by who loves which type of music the most. Use this opportunity to weed out CDs that you no longer like or listen to. Pass them on to charity, to someone who secretly dances around their home to disco in their underwear, or to a store that sells secondhand discs.

If you own a computer, consider using software like iTunes to manage your music from your desktop or laptop. The Windows Media Center PC is also a great way to consolidate all of your music in one place. With some easy-to-install hardware, you can then wirelessly broadcast your favorite music throughout your home. (As with any computer file, however, be sure to regularly do backups of your music in case your system crashes.) Then, presto!, you can toss all of those CDs and use the space for something that can't be stored so efficiently.

If you aren't ready to go digital, put your CDs in binders that will hold and protect them and their liner notes. Discard the jewel cases and see how much space you have saved.

Books and magazines

Books and magazines are almost always a part of the clutter problem in homes that I see. I remember one family that I worked with in Florida where the father was a car enthusiast. He loved anything to do with cars and had about fifteen years of back issues of at least three car magazines in his home. He openly admitted that he didn't read a lot of the magazines and never went back to look at them, but just *having* them in the house reinforced his sense of being a "car guy." It's often the same with books. Just having books in a home can give a home-owner a sense of identity and security, a motivation that has to be addressed before one can deal with the excess.

When I encounter a person who is struggling with too many books or journals or magazines in their home or office, I have another of those simple questions that I ask: What was it that you were purchasing when you bought this reading material? This may sound like a strange question, but the answer is very revealing.

When some people purchase a book, they buy it for their reading pleasure, out of interest in a topic, or because of a rec-ommendation from a family member, friend, or critic. These people are generally able to read a book, digest the information, and use it in whatever way they wish in their lives. Once the book is read and the material understood, these people tend to have no attachment to the book itself.

Then there is a second group who derive a great sense of security and contentment from knowing that they own the book. In many cases, they feel that owning the book is equivalent to owning the *knowledge* in the book, as well. For these individuals, letting go of a book is tantamount to throw-ing that knowledge away—no matter whether they have read the book or not and whether the book still interests them or not.

A couple of years ago, I was working with a woman who had a huge number of books in her home—possibly five or six thousand titles. The books filled every shelf, every flat surface, and most of the house. On average, she bought three or four books a week, far more than she could possibly read. When I tried to discuss letting some of the books go, she became extremely agitated. Eventually she told me why that was impossible: "I don't want someone else to have all this information I've collected. I paid for it and it's mine. Why would I give it away?"

This mind-set is important to recognize when you're downsizing your household's books. Books represent different things to different people. For some they are light entertainment, for others a resource of knowledge and learning, and for others they are reminders of important moments or academic successes. However, when you buy a book, you do not suddenly own the wisdom it contains—all you have bought is words on paper. It's up to you to internalize whatever enlightenment the book has to offer. Without fully grasping this concept, it can be close to impossible to separate oneself from one's books.

Your space dictates how many books you can have

At the beginning of the Charles Dickens novel *David Copperfield,* one of the main characters famously states: "Annual income twenty pounds, annual expenditure nineteen and six, result happiness. Annual income twenty pounds, annual expenditure twenty pounds ought and six, result misery." The character, Mr. Micawber, is instructing the young Copperfield to stay solvent and out of trouble by staying within his means. There's a great lesson here.

When is comes down to it, there is only one simple rule when dealing with books: If they don't fit on your shelves, they shouldn't be in your home. Remember how we learned to "do the math" in Step 2 (see page 88)? To borrow an idea from Dickens, if you have shelving space for 100 books and you have 99 books, you don't have a problem. If, on the other hand, you have shelving space for 100 books and you own 102 books, you have a problem. It's that simple!

You should have no more than the number of books that fit comfortably *on your bookshelves*—not stacked on the floor or on top of the entertainment unit or in boxes in the garage. If your books don't fit on the shelving you have, you have too many and need to either increase the shelving you have or cut down the number of books. And it's probably no surprise that my first recommendation is not to get more shelving!

You may find that reducing the number of books you own is easier said than done. I have been accused of telling people to "get rid of their books"—a charge seemingly as serious as book burning! Again, the honor and respect mandate comes into play here. Someone has labored long and hard over each book you own. If you value books, then treat them so. If not, then understand why you are clinging to them. Why are you suffocating in a dusty, book-filled room? Try to see the book purge as a way of creating a space conducive to reading and the acquisition of knowledge in a way that showcases the volumes you love and honors the collection you have.

Remember the Ratio Rule

Practice the same ratio rule that you used for your movie collection. For every four or five books you keep, remove one from your library. Recycle used books or give them to a library. Repeat until all your books fit on your shelves with room to spare. In the future, when you buy a book, you need to remove a book from your collection.

More on Magazines

Can you believe there are more than twenty-two thousand magazine titles printed in the United States? I can—having been in some homes where three years of back issues of every single one of those twenty-two thousand magazines seem to be piled in the family room! Well—at least it seemed that way at the time. Do you like computers? You can choose from nearly five hundred computer-related magazines. Interested in health and fitness? You've got 350 titles to choose from. And if you just want to sit and ponder the meaning of all of this, there are nearly a dozen philosophy magazines to choose from.

Everybody wants to have the most up-to-date information, but come on, people! There are only about six original ideas in the world and magazine editors keep rotating them—they just change the photos to make you think it's something new! If magazine clutter is your problem, there are some very straightforward ways of dealing with it.

Limit subscriptions

You should have no more than three monthly magazine subscriptions. This may sound tough, but I have yet to meet the person who can deal with the amount of reading material in three magazine subscriptions on top of busy work schedules, a family, the daily newspaper, competing media, and just plain living! It's even harder if some of your favorite magazines are weeklies. Seriously assess how many of the magazines you are getting through each month and cut back accordingly. Don't let your life be the vicarious experience of what others are doing in the glossies. Get out there and make your own news every day!

Limit buildup

Even if you cut back, they just keep coming, don't they? Don't tell yourself you'll get to them one day. Only keep two past issues of any magazine. If you've fallen more than two issues behind—*you will never catch up!* And even if you did manage to get to those back issues, who wants to read or discuss last month's news?

It's this simple—when the third issue of a magazine arrives, throw out the oldest copy. This discipline will help you stay on top of the magazines you have in your home and keep under control the number of back issues cluttering your space.

Don't save catalogs

When you receive an interesting catalog in the mail, look through it immediately. Order anything that you need immediately, then recycle the catalog. If you can't decide about a particular item, don't buy it now and get rid of the catalog. If you're very serious about the item, go to the company's website and bookmark it. But even if you don't go that far, believe me, another identical catalog is coming soon. You won't miss your chance.

Impose order

Keep magazines in one designated spot, like a magazine rack, an in-box, or a coffee table, to ensure they can easily be located and don't roam over the whole house. Magazines arranged in neat piles by title on a coffee table not only suggest order and calm, but also help you to easily see what you still have to read. Put some order into what you read and you'll find yourself getting through a lot more material quicker than you ever have in the past.

MAGAZINE EXCUSES

Don't try to tell me you need to hang on to that magazine. I've heard it all before:

"But this is the greatest turkey gravy recipe I've ever seen— Martha is a genius—I am going to use it at Thanksgiving this year!"

"I am definitely going to build this deck on the back of the house come spring."

"Johnny will probably do a project on Africa one day—I definitely need these copies of *National Geographic.* "

"We will go to Southern California one day—I need this list of quaint bed-and-breakfast places."

If you absolutely must save an article, tear it out, get a scrapbook or a file, and keep it in there. Limit the number of tear-out pages you keep to either the size of the scrapbook or the capacity of the file folder (twenty articles maximum). When you get to twenty, don't let yourself add another until you've thrown one away. Limits and routine—they work every time!

Collectibles

I have lost count of the times someone has looked me in the eye and said, "We can't possibly get rid of those, they're my collectibles!" I am not sure when we stepped into an era that believes plastic NFL sippy cups or NBA bobble heads produced by the millions are collectibles! The word "collectible" has been hijacked by the producers of mass-manufactured crapola. People use the word "collectible" kind of like a "get out of jail free" card—it's become an excuse to hold on to whatever they want. My position is simple—calling a group of like things a "collection" does not automatically give it value or provide a reason for holding on to it.

The line between collectible and clutter is razor thin. Last time I looked on eBay, there were close to *one and a half million items* for sale in their "collectibles" category alone! One and a half million! You call it collectible, I call it barely sellable. Don't get me wrong. I'm sure there's a huge demand for a "RARE! Goebel Toucan Parrot, Tropical Bird Figurine SIGNED!" But what does "collectible" really mean? If you claim an item is a collectible, but it is covered in dust in a trash bag in the corner of the den, or in a water-damaged box in the garage, then I have a hard time believing that item is important to you.

I constantly hear, "But it'll be worth a lot of money one day!" Maybe, but maybe not. Many manufacturers of items labeled "collectibles" have a vested interest in convincing you that there is money to be made sometime in the future. It's not a *purchase*, it's an *investment*. Recently at a well-known college in Texas, the finance department received a fairly large box. Inside was a collection of about one hundred Beanie Babies and a letter. Part of the letter read: "My wife started collecting Beanie Babies in the 1980s and said that the profits from the collection would one day send our son through college. Please accept this box as part payment for my son's tuition." Not all investments pay dividends!

Is your collection really worth keeping? Even when it's impossible to sit in the family room because every chair is covered with Beanie Babies? Remember: How you keep and display your collection is as important as what you collect. Collectibles are deemed such not because of what they're worth or who owns them, but because of the pleasure and joy and value they bring. In your mind you may be a collector, but in reality you may be a hoarder.

REALITY CHECK—COLLECTIONS

It's a collection if:

- it's displayed in a way that makes you proud and shows that you value and honor it.
- looking at it brings you pleasure.
- you enjoy showing it to others.
- it is not an obsession that is damaging your relationships.
- it is not buried under other clutter.
- it doesn't get in the way of living the life you wish you had.

Don't make excuses to keep your collections. Don't hold on to things that you don't love in the hope that they will appreciate in monetary value. Some do, others (generally those mass-produced by the millions) don't. Choose your collection wisely. Or, better yet, "collect" the money instead. In a mutual fund. It's a much wiser way to get that child through college!

Above all, if you have a collection of items, make sure it adds to your happiness. If it's truly meaningful to you, it should be displayed, honored, and respected.

REALITY CHECK—eBAY

More than a marketplace to sell used goods, eBay is one of the best reality checks out there when you're having trouble letting go of something because you think it's worth a lot of money. Going on to eBay tells you exactly what your possessions are worth on the open market. If that "valuable" figurine you inherited from your grandmother is selling for $9.99 on eBay, then it's time to wake up and smell the coffee.

FYI—TRADING ASSISTANTS
There are now companies that will sell your stuff on eBay for you. They're called trading assistants and can be found at www.ebay.com/ta. If you're not tech-savvy or you never seem to find the time to sell things on eBay, it's worth paying the commission to let these folks handle your goods. They take your stuff (gone!), photograph it, sell it online for you, ship it, and send you a check less their commission. No more hoarding boxes and packing materials in anticipation of an eBay selling spree that never happens. No matter how little it turns out your stuff is worth, it's found money: the icing on the cake of your newly clutter-free existence.

Sentimental items

The things we own have incredible power to evoke a memory, to re-create a moment from the past long gone, or to stir up emotions from a previous time. We often hold on to items because they have these strong memories attached. When we have trouble letting go of an object, it's usually the memory, rather than the item itself, that we are frightened of losing. You may not be able to articulate this fear, but in your heart you know that the power the item has over you is profound. This situation is not at all unusual. When clutter is sentimental, you need to figure out two things: first, how to separate the memory from the item, and second, how to preserve the memory in a way that honors and respects it. This process takes the power away from the object in a way that is really liberating and enables you to live your life without the sense of fear and worry of future loss.

Darlene, the mother of three children ages five, eight, and twelve, still had their baby crib in the master bedroom. She was unable to let go of it because it represented so many wonderful memories for her. Here's how I helped her reframe her attitude to the crib.

Step 1: We talked about her kids, and how the best memories weren't limited to the past. They had big milestones ahead. New memories—big birthdays, puberty, graduations, and transformations were down the road for all of them. Once she grasped this idea, it was easier for her to let go of some of the past. She was able to look forward to an exciting future of great new memories and experiences with her children.

Step 2: We talked about what she could do with the crib. It turned out she had a neighbor who was not very well off and was adopting a child from China. When Darlene offered her neighbor the crib, she gladly accepted it. She also promised to give Darlene a photo of the adopted child in the crib. Darlene found a whole new source of pleasure from the crib—the pleasure of knowing that it would go to a good home, be put to great use, and be valued by someone else who was building a family.

DEAR PETER:

When my grandmother died, my mother sent me all her china. It arrived carefully packed in six huge boxes. I knew I wouldn't use it (we love our wedding china), so it sat in our garage, still packaged, awaiting our next move. I finally unpacked it—it was taking up so much space—so then it was taking up space in our dining room. But we still never used it. Every time I looked at it, I resented the space it was taking up, but it was my grandmother's wedding china! Finally I called my mother and told her I didn't like it and didn't want to keep it. To my surprise, she didn't care at all! I took it to an eBay trading assistant, and they said it wasn't worth enough to sell. My grandmother's beloved china—worthless! When I picked it up at the trading assistant storefront, I looked at it and imagined my life without it. Nothing would be different. I drove straight to Goodwill and never looked back. I just told myself what I've heard you say a million times: The thing isn't the person. The china wasn't my grandmother, or her memory. It was just some old, cheap china.

Remembering without saving

How can you let go of a physical item while still honoring the memory?

Textile memories. Are you having trouble letting go of your grandmother's mildewed wedding dress or grandfather's moth-eaten army uniform? Cut a piece of the material and frame it next to a photo of your grandparent wearing the article. Write out a memory of your grandparent to include in the frame.

Family photos. Face it, nobody wants to look at your family photos. We all take photos, but few of us are photographers. You're lucky if a tenth of the photos you take are quality photos. So here's what you do: Get a nice photo album and for every event you go to—wedding, family outing, weekend getaway—pick the best photo of the lot and put it in the album. Next to it, on a piece of paper, write a paragraph about the event. Put the album in a public, prominent place in your home. That album becomes a greatest hits collection, a CliffsNotes chronology of important events. An album like this is a pleasure to look through, for you, and for your visitors. Of course, if you can go digital, by all means do so. You'll quickly see how infrequently you actually bother to look at your photos, even when they're right there on your computer taking up so little space.

Photos of children and children's artwork. Choose a few easy-to-use frames. Hang them in a prominent spot in your home. Fill them with your current favorite snapshot or piece of art. Every few months, swap in a new photo or painting. Move the retired favorite to an album. You can do the same thing by slipping photos under Plexiglas on your desk.

Any of the above. Gather all the items you are keeping for the memories, but never plan to use. Set up a video camera on a tripod. Hold up the items, one at a time, while talking to the camera. When your kids are older you can give them this video journal as an enduring record of what's most important—the memories, not the stuff.

REALITY CHECK—MORE CLUTTER-FREE STRATEGIES FOR HONORING MEMORIES

- Talk about the item—without touching it—and tell the most memorable story you have of it. Celebrate the memory attached to the item.
- Take a photo of the item (or a clipping of the fabric if appropriate) and place it in a scrapbook with a short narrative telling the story of that item or the strongest memory you associate with it.
- Make a pillow out of sentimental fabric, or use the fabric to cover an album that you fill with photos of the person who wore the item.
- Use shadow boxes or picture frames to display important sentimental items.
- Pass items to someone who you know will use them and needs them more than you do—another family member, a charity, a neighbor. (Just be careful not to pass on the burden of unwanted clutter.)

Room 4

Home Office

THE HOME OFFICE has become a standard area of our homes. Many people use this space to work from home, to handle the day-to-day business of running a household, to answer mail and pay bills, and as a place for their computers. While we'd all like the home office to be a model of efficiency, for many it seems to be a special kind of magnet that attracts every conceivable piece of paper that comes into the home: books, magazines, bills, receipts, tax necessities, product warranties, letters, files, and reams of personal must-keep data that have no clear home other than on a desk, chair, or floor in the corner of the room.

THINK IT THROUGH

Office clutter is almost always a paper problem. What's amazing is that if you think about the paper that fills your office—the books, magazines, files, and mail—you'll realize that most of it is stuff you'll never use again. As we work on the paper problem areas, you'll learn to assess how much of that paper to keep and how it is best kept.

SET IT UP

- Refer to your Room Function Chart and have everyone sign on.
- Establish zones for the different activities that take place in the home office.
- Remove what *doesn't* belong in the room.

MAKE IT HAPPEN

Create "zones" in your home office for paperwork

We've already done this for other rooms in your home and now it's time to do it in your home office. Make sure that you have designated places for the main types of paper that live in this space:

- Mail—unopened or needing some response
- Magazine storage
- Bills and receipts
- Important personal information and files

Mail and bill-paying should be located close together. Envelopes, stamps, your checkbook, and other items that you need on a frequent basis should be close at hand. Having clear zones means more efficient work and a clear home for all like items.

FYI—ORGANIZING YOUR CREDIT CARDS

All credit cards have emergency contact numbers on their reverse side—however, this is not much use if you lose the card or if it is stolen. Place all your credit cards on a photocopying machine and make copies of the front and rear of the cards. Place the copies in a safe place. If your cards are lost or stolen you have a complete record of their numbers.

Keep all horizontal surfaces clear

The way you feel about a space is set the moment you step into it. Set the mood for an efficient workspace and keep your office uncluttered by ensuring that any desk surface, countertop, or table is kept clear of paperwork and clutter. If you don't start piles, they can't grow.

Work efficiently

Have the right tools for the job! Invest in a great desk chair. Make sure that your desk is the right height, your lighting is adequate, and you have a notebook and pen next to the phone. Simple things count—and increase your productivity.

Embrace the digital world

In this age of computers and the Internet, be sure to use both software and hardware to your best advantage. Organize your files clearly, delete old computer files regularly, back up your important files, and, wherever possible, use the Internet to conduct business, pay bills, and so on. Online banking and bill paying can help reduce paper clutter and remove some of the end-of-month stress from your life.

PAPER

I recently worked with Dean, a financial consultant with more than twenty years of experience who knows more about money and investments than anyone I know. He came to me because he needed help organizing his "financial articles," as he put it. It turned out that Dean had amassed more than ten thousand industry-related articles over the course of his career. Although he clipped and put aside as many as twenty articles a week, he never managed to read more than a third of them. When Dean saw that collecting the articles was more about his fear of missing important information than anything else, he was able to reduce the number of articles he clipped without feeling constantly stressed about what he might be missing. And the side benefit was since he spent less time clipping, he had more time to spend reading the articles that really mattered!

Remember when we were told that the advent of the computer would mark the beginning of a paperless society? Wouldn't you like to get your hands on the guy who made that prediction? Like it or not, paper is here to stay. The home office is a breeding ground for flammable clutter: paperwork, files, family records, books. Paper has a habit of sitting around, waiting for you to do something with it. It's either waiting to be read, or waiting to be paid, or waiting to be filed. Although paper comes in many different forms, one thing is definitely true—the secret is managing the paper before the paper starts managing you!

MAIL

FYI ON MAIL

Coupons, bills, invitations, junk mail. Every day the mail is a project in and of itself. It has been estimated that the average American receives close to fifty thousand pieces of mail during his or her life, of which about a third is junk mail. Worse still, each of us spends an average of eight months in the course of a lifetime going through that junk mail! That's why you should do any and everything you can to handle your mail more efficiently.

Household mail—it needs a home

We all receive important information through the mail—much of which requires some kind of response to ensure the smooth running of our homes and our lives. Bills need to be paid, invitations require a response, and inquiries from the bank or a government office need replies. Streamlining this process takes a lot of unnecessary worry out of responding on time and ensures that your household business is attended to in a timely fashion. You cannot hope to have a smooth-functioning household if you don't have your mail under control.

In a small town in North Carolina, I worked with Matt, a guy who was so overwhelmed with mail that it was close to comical—even he dissolved into laughter when we started talking about it. Matt had decided that he had to keep all mail that came into his house. There wasn't a lot of logic to this, but it was a belief that Matt had stuck to for quite a few years. However, while he felt that the junk mail could be stored in an ever-increasing number of large plastic trash cans in his home, he felt that the most important pieces of mail—paid bills, old credit card statements, any official correspondence—should be kept in a more secure location. He decided that the most secure place he could think of was his car. So Matt had a house overflowing with junk mail and a car bursting with personal mail. This all seemed like a fine idea until late one night when Matt swerved to avoid an animal on the road and, blinded by flying paper, wound up driving his car into a large pond just off Highway 70.

Take it from me—the backseat of your car is not the ideal place to keep your mail. Nor is the bathroom, family room, kitchen counter, or bedside table. Consider setting up a simple file tray or basket to hold all incoming mail that needs a response. This way you will easily be able to locate any mail that you have and can be sure that you are responding to everything that needs your attention. Get into the habit of always placing mail in this designated spot, and train everyone else in the household to do the same. It may sound trivial but it will save you hours of frustrated searching and ensure no more late payments or lost invitations.

Junk mail

Junk mail is your enemy! Imagine there is a knock at your door. You open the door to see a man with a can of spray paint in his hand. Do you: a) invite him in, or b) slam the door in his face? This is how you should think of junk mail! It's an intruder waiting to get inside and wreak havoc. Junk mail is the bane of most people's existence. But like it or not, it's here to stay. It's how we manage it that is important.

MORE FYI ON MAIL
More than 100 million trees are needed to produce the nearly 4.5 million tons of junk mail that's mailed every year in this country, nearly half of which is never opened.

I am only half joking when I tell people that the moment you let a piece of junk mail touch any flat surface inside your home, you might as well pack up, move out, and sell the house! Once inside your home, junk mail has the capacity to reproduce in the dark until it covers all flat surfaces. If you think this is crazy, please give me some other explanation for the fact that every flat surface in most of the houses I see (maybe yours?) is layered in junk mail?

Treat junk mail like the intruder it is. Wherever possible, do not let junk mail into your home. Place a recycle bin for the junk mail somewhere handy and be sure to deposit those annoying envelopes efficiently. Shred any correspondence containing personal information.

Another strategy is to stop the junk mail from ever reaching your home. This is a little more time-consuming, but well worth the effort. There are specific things you can do to reduce the volume of unwanted mail that you receive.

STRATEGIES FOR MINIMIZING JUNK MAIL

- Contact the Direct Marketing Association by e-mail or regular mail. Visit their website at www.dmaconsumers .org and go to Consumer Assistance. Or send a postcard to the DMA, Mail Preference Service, P.O. Box 643, Carmel, New York 10512. Ask them to "activate the mail preference service." You need to list your complete name, address, and zip code. Listing with the mail preference service will stop 75 percent of all national mailings. It may take a couple of months before you notice a difference in the volume of junk mail, but it is well worth doing.

- Avoid receiving all those annoying credit card offers that swamp all of us. Call toll-free, twenty-four hours a day: 888-5OPT-OUT (888-567-8688) to have your name removed from the list of the major credit organizations. Follow the computer prompts and choose to have your name removed for two years or forever.

continued

- Insist that your name and address not be sold when you sign up for a new catalog, buy a new product, or any time you provide your personal details as part of a business transaction. Save a tree, control the clutter, and save a little sanity. Every little bit helps!

Bills and receipts

As much as we hate them, bills are the most important mail we receive. Personal correspondence is definitely more meaningful, but these days most of that happens via e-mail. If bills are not paid on time, credit card companies have no hesitation in slapping us with late fees. Credit card debt can sneak up on you, and it's a nasty beast that eats your funds faster than you can earn them. If utility bills are left unpaid, you can find yourself without a phone or other basic services. Not being on top of your bills costs in ways beyond the financial. It causes stress and tension, both for you and others in your household. It can seriously impact your reputation, your credit rating, and, in the long run, jeopardize future opportunities for mortgages or car loans.

DEAR PETER:
"Get rid of the trash to make room for the treasures."
"Let the things that are important take center stage." I walk around my house cleaning and saying these things to myself. I realize what is truly important to me and what is easily tossed. An indoor grill that I had not used in over four years saw its way to the garbage and I made room for the antique mixer my great aunt had given to me before she died, which I adore. The cheap mirror I picked up on vacation four years ago left the house in a pile of rubble to make room for a new-and-improved message board with an actual place for hubby to put the

incoming mail and a place for me to hang my keys! Then, instead of a denim bag on the back of the door for the bills, I purchased a real bill organizer with dated slots. And it works! Yesterday I paid the cable bill the same day we got it!

Use technology to your advantage

Try to pay as many bills online as you can. Consider software like Quicken to track all bills, assist in online payments, and help in the yearly preparation of your taxes. Most companies will accept an automatic bill-paying schedule, or you can simply set up your online account and then check the bills to ensure their accuracy each month before approving the money transfer.

Streamline the process

Keep all of your mail in one central location. It should be close to or on the same desk as your computer. When it comes time to pay your bills, you should be able to do so quickly and efficiently—whether online or by mail. In addition, keep all necessary bill-paying items—stamps, envelopes, and checkbook—together in the same place near the mail and computer. No more time wasted trying to find envelopes, stamps, or your checkbook. The bills are painful enough, why take any longer than you absolutely have to?

Maintain a system

Many people are uncomfortable with shredding or discarding paid bills. I have seen homes where every receipt and paid bill from the previous ten years is strewn throughout the house. If you want to keep paid bills and/or receipts, you need to keep the paperwork under control. Start by purchasing a twelve-month expanding file. When you pay bills for, say, June, place them in the June section of the file. You'll come back to June twelve months later. If you haven't needed to look at the bills in that time, it's highly unlikely that you'll ever need them again. Shred them. The same system works for receipts. Another simple, very low-tech solution to organizing receipts is to use two bankers' spikes. Get in the habit of cleaning receipts out of your wallet or purse daily. Place receipts on one of the spikes as they come in. When one spike is full, start the other. If you haven't needed any of the receipts in the time it takes you to fill a spike, chances are you never will. When you fill up the second spike, throw out all the receipts on the first. (See **Tax Stuff** on page 151 for what bills and receipts to keep.)

These methods ensure that the huge amount of paperwork that bills and receipts amount to over a year can easily be managed, quickly accessed, and kept in a tidy and organized way. It's simple—all it takes is commitment and discipline to make the system work.

FILING

The road to good organization is paved with discarded filing systems. File cabinets can be sneaky. They masquerade as organization solutions, but while they're better than random stacks of disorderly papers, they don't automatically solve the problem. Why? Because part of the problem, strangely, is that a file cabinet can hold so much paper that the temptation is to fill it, or to file everything. This is a mistake! Remember that 80 percent of what goes into a filing cabinet never sees the light of day again. Be judicious about what you file and schedule a time each year when you go through your files to get rid of those things that are outdated or no longer needed.

Invest in a good filing system
Use a stable, well-made filing cabinet and consider one of the commercially available systems like File Solutions or Freedom Filer that help to keep paperwork in order by providing pre-

labeled files that cover every aspect of home operation imaginable. These systems organize and manage your personal and family papers and take any guesswork out of setting up an easy-to-use and complete system.

Clearly label your files in a logical way that enables you to quickly and efficiently retrieve any information you need. If you're ambitious, color code them like the professionals do—whatever you do, choose a system that will work for your particular situation. Once you file something, it can be very easy to totally forget where it is, or even that it exists. A good filing system ensures that you can quickly and confidently lay your hands on any important piece of paperwork without raising a sweat.

SUGGESTED FILING CATEGORIES

Automotive—maintenance and repair details, warranties, purchase details.

Education—copies of transcripts or degrees. Report cards, school details.

Financial—credit cards, bank statements, investments, tax returns, and retirement funds.

Health and medical—details of coverage, medical practitioner contact information, dental records, tests performed.

Home and real estate—house purchase details, home improvement ideas, copies of receipts for work done on property, investment property details.

Insurance—house and contents policies, car insurance, life insurance, disability insurance, or any other policies you may have. Paperwork related to any claims you have filed.

Legal—important documents such as passports, birth and marriage certificates, copies of wills and trusts.

Work—employment contracts, résumés, work benefit program details.

continued

Taxes—one file for each year's return and supporting paperwork.

The above categories can be expanded or subdivided to meet your specific needs. Some additional categories:

Child care services	*Pets*
Entertainment	*Retirement planning*
Events/birthdays	*Travel and vacations*
Family history	*Appliance and other manuals*
Food/wine	*Warranties*

Don't file everything

I recently worked with a family where the mother had a fear of losing any important piece of paperwork. The problem was that everything seemed important to her; she didn't know where to draw the line. When we started looking at the immaculately kept filing system, I discovered that she had even filed receipts for meals from fast-food places for the last twelve years! Choose what you file carefully. If in doubt, speak to an accountant or other financial professional who can offer some advice on what to keep and what to let go. Consider marking items with a "keep until" date so that you have a clear idea of when to discard time-sensitive paperwork. Remember—it's likely that you're only going to need a fifth of what you file anyway, so choose carefully before sliding that paper into your file cabinet where it may linger, completely unnecessarily, for years.

Be efficient

Keep frequently used files (bank statements, car insurance) handy so you can quickly and easily access important information. The top drawer of your filing cabinet should contain the files you need the most, including receipts, bank statements, and other paperwork you'll want for this year's tax return. Store old tax files in a less accessible place (you'll only need them again if you're audited). Consider assigning a drawer to each family member and one drawer for common paperwork. Make labels for the outside of each drawer of your filing cabinet so you can see at a glance what that drawer contains.

If you don't need it—get rid of it

Don't let your filing cabinet become a paper burial ground. Cull your files once a year to get rid of outdated and unwanted items. It is imperative to purge your filing cabinets on a regular basis for two reasons—first, to get rid of old things, but also to refresh your memory of what is actually in there. Trust me—it can be a surprising exercise!

Tax Stuff

The concern that Uncle Sam may come knocking on our door to conduct a tax audit strikes fear into our hearts. Keeping your financial records in order and knowing that the supporting documents are easily accessible should allay that fear enormously. The government provides clear guidelines for what records we need to keep—it's our job to make sure we're organized enough to meet those standards and it's really not that difficult to do.

FYI—IRS SPECIFICATIONS

You can download a publication of the IRS about what paperwork to keep. Go to www.irs.gov and search for Publication No. 552.

Here are some broad and fairly conservative guidelines for managing your bills and financial records for tax season and audits. My official disclaimer is that you shouldn't take my word for it and should check with your own accountant or financial advisor in your state to verify that this information is up-to-date and accurate for your location and situation.

TAX TRASH CALENDAR

Every month:

- Toss out ATM, bank deposit slips, and credit card receipts (unless you may need them for audit purposes) after you have checked them against your bank or credit card statements.
- Toss out receipts for minor purchases—unless there is a warranty or refund involved.

Every year:

- Toss out your monthly bank and credit card statements (unless you require proof of deductions for taxation purposes)—most credit card companies provide a year-end summary that you can retain.
- Toss out monthly mortgage statements provided you receive a year-end summary of your account.
- Toss out pay stubs after they are checked against your W-2 or 1099.
- Toss out your W-2 and 1099 forms from seven years ago and earlier.
- Toss out canceled checks and receipts or annual statements for:

  Mortgage interest from seven years ago and earlier.

  Property taxes from seven years ago and earlier.

  Deductible business expenses or other tax-deductible expenses from seven years ago and earlier.

Keep indefinitely:

- Annual tax returns.
- Year-end summary statements from financial institutions.
- Receipts for the purchase of any investments you own.
- Receipts for home-improvement costs or major purchases that may be needed for insurance claims or similar.

REALITY CHECK—CREDIT CARD DEBT

It may not seem obvious, but there is a connection between debt and clutter. I'm not talking about home, school, or car loans. Those loans tend to have reasonable interest rates, but credit card debt is a real devil, and it is always the result of inappropriate acquisition of goods. The average American family owes $9,200 in credit card debt. Some of us get sucked into credit card debt when we're young, unemployed, and/or vulnerable. Who can blame us when companies are aggressively marketing credit cards to college students and bankruptcy filers? With credit cards at their disposal in college, kids try to duplicate the standard of living they had with their families. They develop a sense that they can acquire whatever they want. Kids come out of school and instead of starting from scratch, they are starting out with debt, and the worst kind: credit card debt. And once you've got a little debt, it's a hard habit to break.

When it comes to managing your credit cards, you need to establish routines and set limits. Sound familiar? It's the same thing I told you to teach your children. Limited space equals limited toys. Limited funds equals limited spending. Trust me, no matter how much you want that stereo or that new car, excess spending will bring you more grief in the long run.

SCRAPBOOKING AND CRAFTING

Scrapbooking has become incredibly popular in the last few years. It's estimated that some twenty-three million people now do scrapbooking in the United States. That's almost one in every four households! The number of people who engage in some kind of hobby or craft is similar. Most of my clients have had crafting clutter; many have had more scrapbooking materials than I want to think about. Remember that owning the crafting supplies or the scrapbooking materials doesn't automatically make you a crafter or a scrapbooker. What are the end results of owning these materials? What are you making? Is it a source of pleasure and relaxation or one more stressful thing in your home that you just don't seem to get to?

DEAR PETER:

I happen to be a fabricaholic and have over twenty banker boxes of various fabrics. This past weekend I promised myself I'd pare it down by 50 percent and actually ended up with only seven boxes to keep. The rest I arranged to give to a gal at work who is a single mom, loves to sew, and has small children. She's thrilled and I'm much better off.

If you choose a craft or hobby, then make sure it's something you really enjoy. Do it because you want to, not because others expect it of you or because it's something you once liked or because you don't want those materials you bought to go to waste. Just as you should choose the life you want, it's also your choice how you spend your free time.

Have limits

About a year ago I worked with Jan and Thomas, a couple who described themselves as "avid hobbyists" and who wanted some help in organizing their crafting and hobby supplies. Their home was overflowing with every imaginable item that could be needed for the many crafts they said they loved. Hers: knitting, decoupage, quilting, doll painting, pottery, jewelry making, and watercolor painting. His: model airplane building, remote control car construction and racing, black-and-white photography, woodworking, and metal sculpting. When we started going through the hobby materials, one thing became obvious quickly. Each of them had at least fifteen "projects" going at that time, some of which dated back nearly ten years! Jan and Thomas would have been better off owning a hobby and craft store—they had enough stock.

Clutter is one of the biggest blocks to creativity there is. You cannot think creatively when you are overwhelmed with the tools or materials of your craft—it just doesn't work that way. Jan and Thomas agreed to cut their hobbies back to three each and to have no more than three projects going at any one time. Before starting a new project, they had to finish or discard an old one. By maintaining these limits, they opened up their physical space and experienced a huge surge in their creative energy and enthusiasm for their crafts.

Remember the zones

If you enjoy a craft or love scrapbooking, you need an area dedicated to your hobby where you can maintain all of the items you need to complete the project you are working on. Once you have established your creative zone, designate areas for all of the supplies, materials, and equipment you may need. Keep this area clean and organized so that you can easily return to a project, even if you only have a short period of time to devote to it. Most important, make sure you put away anything you've used and clean up after yourself. This makes the area an attractive place to return to and establishes a routine that will boost your creativity.

Live your life

Leanne had one room in her home that she called "scrapbooking central." It was here that she hoped to assemble detailed memory albums for her three young children. The problem was that Leanne had purchased so many supplies, and had so little time, that every time she went near "scrapbooking central" she felt overwhelmed by the clutter and guilty that she had barely started albums for her two younger children. Leanne had completely unrealistic expectations for how much scrapbooking she could handle.

You have to live your life. Scrapbooking can be a wonderful way to preserve memories, but without a sense of balance, preserving the memories can get in the way of creating them. You cannot preserve every single memory. Take only the best, the most exciting, and the most memorable moments as your starting point. If you have time to create scrapbooks for these moments, then consider broadening your goals. Only keep the supplies you need for the project you are working on and be sure that scrapbooking or any other hobby does not become an end in itself.

WRAPPING PAPER

Finally, I should admit upfront that I am not a big fan of wrapping paper—well, at least not what most people think of when they use the term. I am at a loss to understand when wrapping paper became such a national obsession. In some homes I have encountered more than a hundred rolls of different types of wrapping paper—paper for Christmas or Hanukkah, for babies or brides, for weddings and anniversaries, for children and older persons, and even for dogs or cats. Personalizing gifts by using distinctive wrapping paper isn't necessarily a bad thing, but if your home is overrun with wrapping paper, then it may well be time to do something about it.

There is a simple and elegant way to manage the wrapping of gifts. Remember this principle: More is not necessarily better! Purchase a roll of good quality brown paper and high quality ribbons of three colors—black, red, and white. Wrap all your gifts in this simple brown paper and decorate with any selection of the ribbons. Brown paper too dull for you? Use the same approach selecting your "signature" color. This minimal approach will mean that your gifts will always stand out and that you will not have to spend a fortune on wrapping paper. Best of all, these supplies take up negligible room. Elegance in simplicity—it really does work!

Room 5

Kitchen

THE KITCHEN IS THE NERVE CENTER of any home. It is usually the first port of call when anyone comes into a home and often the place where most of the action takes place—chatting, cooking, eating, maybe doing homework, or even paying the bills. When you add all that activity to the inevitable mess of preparing, serving, and eating meals, the kitchen can be a tough place to keep organized and clean. Try looking at your kitchen in a new way. Stop and think about how much energy you waste in looking for things. Consider how you move in that space and what you need to get the job done. With that in mind, let's tackle one of the most challenging spaces in your home.

THINK IT THROUGH

The principle notion behind kitchen cleanup is that there's no such thing as saving for later. Food goes bad. Dishes get used. Everything else goes. Now, of course I understand that there are special food occasions. As we clean out the kitchen, I need you to be realistic about these special food occasions, making sure they aren't special food occasion *fantasies*. The kitchen is all about form and function. You know what you use all the time; keep those things close at hand and everything else out of the way. You need counter space more than you need that fondue pot, so make sure you treat "room to work" like an appliance that deserves plenty of counter space. And if those special occasions truly exist, the materials you need for them should be less accessible and properly labeled.

SET IT UP

- Refer to your Room Function Chart and have everyone sign on.
- Establish zones for the different activities that take place in the kitchen.
- Remove what *doesn't* belong in the room.

MAKE IT HAPPEN

Keep flat surfaces clear

Keeping flat surfaces clear is perhaps the single most important thing to keep in mind for your kitchen—as it is for any room in the house. A clear countertop makes any kitchen look more organized. Once the flat surfaces start to disappear under clutter, you lose your motivation to keep the area organized and you open the area to attracting more dust and dirt, further compounding the clutter problem. Consider flat surfaces your preparation area—not your storage area!

Work around the "magic triangle"

Think of the area formed by your sink, refrigerator, and oven or stovetop as the "magic triangle" of your kitchen. This triangle is sacred ground—the focus of food preparation, cleanup, and serving. Anything that is central to your daily food preparation (pots, wooden spoons, food storage bags, everyday dishes, etc.) should be located in or on the sides of this triangle. Nothing else should be in that area. One step out of the triangle is stuff you use regularly, but infrequently: food processor, mixer, specialty pots. One step farther is stuff you seldom use: bread maker, turkey pan, Christmas cookie cutters. By organizing your kitchen in this way, you will find yourself moving efficiently in the space with minimum movement for maximum return. By having important and frequently used items close, you will save an enormous amount of time and energy in your kitchen.

Think of your kitchen in terms of zones

The "magic triangle" concept is strongly supported by the idea of establishing specific zones in your kitchen. Create four main zones or areas in your kitchen: the preparation area, the cooking center, the eating area, and the cleanup area. The preparation area is near the sink and needs plenty of free counter space and easy access to knives and cutting boards. The cooking center is near the oven or stovetop and needs easy access to pots, pans, cooking utensils, and spices. The eating area needs clear space and easy access to eating utensils, napkins, salt and pepper, and other condiments. And finally, the cleanup area needs room to wash and dry dishes that don't go in the dishwasher. Organize items according to these work zones and it will immediately make your kitchen more efficient.

All roads lead to the kitchen

In many households, the kitchen is the central place where family members tend to leave anything and everything. Coats, school bags, mail, toys, homework, notices—you name it.

Space permitting, install sturdy hooks into the wall where bags and backpacks can be hung. Label them clearly for each member of the household. You might also attach a small bag or place a labeled bin on the floor under each hook—toys, mail, or other items can be placed here for each person. This is also a great area to hang car keys and purses so that they can easily be grabbed as you leave the house.

Only keep what you need and use

THE ONE-MONTH CARDBOARD BOX TEST

Not sure what you use and what you don't? Here is a tried and true way to find out. Empty the contents of your kitchen utensil drawers into a cardboard box. For one month, only put a utensil back into the drawer if you take it out of the box to use it. At the end of the month seriously consider discarding everything that's still in the cardboard box. Face it: If it's still in the box after four weeks, you don't need it!

Kitchens attract a ton of useless but seemingly "must-have" gadgets and gizmos. Tune into late-night infomercials if you don't believe me! The first step to getting organized is to seriously pare down the amount of food, dishes, and appliances in your kitchen. Discard those items that have outlived their usefulness. Do you really need to keep that slow cooker just because it was a Christmas present? It's taking up valuable counter space. And those specialty pots and pans, egg slicers, apple corers, melon ballers, and who knows what—do you *really* need and use them? One other thing—like it or not, that fondue pot needs to go!

LEAST-USED KITCHEN ITEMS

BIG:	SMALL:
Fondue pot	Egg slicer
Bread-making machine	Apple corer
Crepe maker	Pizza cutter
Ice cream machine	Grapefruit spoons
Vegetable juicer	Anything costing $19.99
Crock-Pot	on late-night television.
Waffle iron	
Propane torch	
Cookie press	
Banana-ripening rack	
Pizza stone	

Keep like items together

Whether it's plates, pots and pans, or food items, be sure to keep similar items in the same place. Following this rule will also save time and money as you can quickly and easily see what items you already have in stock and avoid overpurchasing.

Claim vertical space in your kitchen

Make use of the space you have. Expand the available space in your cupboards by using a lazy Susan, ministep shelves, racks, and even "back-of-door" shelving systems to hold extra items. These are easy and inexpensive solutions that will help you avoid losing items in the back of deep cupboards. Try creative ways to use the wall space—hang a notice board to control paper clutter and ensure everyone has a place to post important notes and notices.

Regularly check food cupboards

Schedule time every six months to check the contents of cupboards and every three months to discard old food or perishables. Place all of your cooking and baking ingredients onto the kitchen countertop so that you can get an idea of how much and what you have. Put like ingredients next to each other. This regular review will mean that the kitchen clutter will not get on top of you again! When you buy new canned and boxed items, place them behind the ones that are already in the cupboard. This will guarantee that your food is rotated and you will avoid having anything past its use-by date.

If you're wondering how long those foods in your pantry will last, an excellent site to check out the shelf life of pretty much any foodstuff is http://www.msnbc.com/OnAir/nbc/Dateline/Food/shelf.asp.

The need to regularly check items is also true for food in your refrigerator and freezer. Check regularly to ensure that you are not keeping food beyond its use-by date. Frozen foods do not keep forever, so sort through those frozen blocks at the bottom of your freezer. Any time you put something into your freezer, label it clearly with the contents and the date of freezing. If you can't remember what an item is, chances are that it's time for it to go! The Department of Agriculture has a great site with tips for freezing and keeping food items at http://www.fsis.usda.gov/Fact_Sheets/Focus_On_Freezing/index.asp.

Consider a clear solution

Think about investing in clear plastic containers or a glass-shelved refrigerator that will help you find what you are looking for and see when it's time to stock up again. Clear containers also let you keep like things together.

FYI—SHELF LIFE

Keep track of the expiration dates on bottled and canned goods. Generally, these items can be safely kept, unopened, for about a year. Refrigerate after opening, being sure to transfer unused canned goods to an airtight container. Dried goods such as rice and pasta are best used within a year of purchase and should be stored in an airtight container once opened. Most spices should be discarded after twelve months as they tend to lose their flavor after that time. Store baking supplies in airtight containers in a cool, dark cupboard for up to one year.

Clean as you go

More so than in any other room in the house, it's important to get into the habit in your kitchen of fully completing a task. If you are stirring a pot and splash food on the counter, wipe it up. If you are clearing the table, put the dishes in the dishwasher immediately. At the end of the meal, wash the pots and pans and rinse out the sink. This simple routine of cleaning as you go and completing a task fully will help to maintain order and cleanliness in your kitchen.

DRAWER BY DRAWER

Pots and pans

Storing pots and pans is awkward and space-consuming. That's why they sell those ceiling racks that allow you to hang pots attractively above your head. Another handy solution is a corner cupboard with a rotating tray that allows you to spin the contents until you find the cookware you need. But if neither of

these solutions works for you, your pots can be a storage night-
mare. Go through them occasionally. See what has migrated to
the back of the cupboard. Just because it's a perfectly good
stockpot, if you never use it, you don't have to keep it. And remember: If you have large cookware that you only use for occa-
sional entertaining, store it high up and out of the busiest areas
of your kitchen.

Utensils

Regular forks, knives, and spoons don't cause much trouble,
but most households have at least one drawer devoted to cooking utensils—everything from wooden spoons and spatulas to
garlic presses and meat thermometers. If you can, designate a
drawer near the stove for utensils you use exclusively for cooking. Keep knives near your prep area. Generally, you need no
more than five high-quality sharp knives for food preparation. If
your drawers are loaded with more than this, pare them down
(pun intended). Install a magnetic strip on the wall of your
kitchen next to the food preparation area and you'll always have
quick and easy access to your knives.

Food storage containers

Those plastic food storage containers seem so practical. You can
never have too many, right? Wrong. Use a couple of small pieces
of masking tape to seal all your containers. As you use them,
you'll break the seal. After six months (preferably encompass-
ing Thanksgiving), get rid of the containers that still have un-
broken masking tape seals.

Cookbooks

Find an inexpensive scrapbook or file to hold all of those fantastic recipes you find in magazines or are given by friends. Keep

the scrapbook with other cookbooks in a central place in your kitchen. Go through your cookbooks and discard any you haven't opened in a year. If, by chance, you do one day need a recipe for Bavarian apple strudel custard cake, there is always the Internet.

Christine's kitchen was overflowing with specialty cookware and gourmet cookbooks, few of which she used and none of which she could bring herself to let go of. She loved cooking shows and watched them all the time, jotting down recipes and making plans for elaborate family feasts. When we worked to declutter and organize her kitchen, Christine admitted that success in the kitchen represented excellence in homemaking for her. To let go of any part of her kitchen was scary because it meant risking failure. She dealt with this fear by first writing down her family's favorite meals, then identifying the utensils and items she needed to prepare them. This way, it was easier for her to let go of most of the specialty items and cookbooks that she never used.

COOKBOOK POST-IT TEST

If you have too many cookbooks for your kitchen, try this simple test. Every time you use a recipe from a cookbook, mark the page with a Post-it. At the end of eighteen months, get rid of books that have no Post-its. Of course, if you have space for extra cookbooks that you never use, no problem. Go ahead and enjoy not using them.

Junk drawer

Lots of kitchens have a "catch-all" drawer. What's in here? It's always a surprise. Soy sauce packets from carryout, rubber bands, pennies, matches, pushpins, a stray refrigerator magnet. I'm only going to say this once: No. Junk. Drawer. Do I make myself clear?

Divide and conquer

Even when you declutter all of the items that you really don't need or use in your kitchen, it can be a task to keep drawers organized. You can keep like things together in your drawers easier by installing inexpensive drawer dividers or small boxes. Simply being able to see different categories of items sitting together in your kitchen drawers will make it a pleasure to go looking for anything and it will be much simpler to know where everything lives in your space.

Creative solutions

Most people tend to think of drawers as the main storage areas in a kitchen. A butcher's block on wheels can be a great way to get items out of drawers and close to where you use them. These kinds of butcher's blocks can be wheeled around the kitchen and so increase the amount of flat area you have for meal preparation. They also come with hanging hooks and space for storing kitchen tools and food items.

REALITY CHECK—WEDDINGS

When you get married, you can expect a huge number of gifts as your loved ones follow the tradition of helping you set up your home. For whatever reason, tool sets and electronic equipment don't seem to be the most popular wedding presents. Most of the gifts are kitchen-centric—china, silver, pots and pans, and appliances. The registry is a great way to avoid getting stuff you won't use. But inevitably, peo-

continued

ple buy gifts "off registry" and you get stuff you don't like. You feel obligated to keep it. On top of that, you inevitably register for stuff you never end up using. At the top of the list are fondue pots, vases, glass serving platters for dips and chips, punch bowls, and wine carafes. Just remember: A gift is not an obligation. If you can do it discreetly, return what you won't use. Otherwise, donate or sell it. If you must wait until the giver visits your home and sees his or her gift in active use, fine, but when the time is right, you guessed it: Out it goes.

Room 6

Dining Room

IN NEWER HOUSES the dining space is often part of the kitchen. Nevertheless, there is a dining area in every home. At some point we seem to have lost the concept of dining, and have replaced it with an interest solely in the mechanics of eating. When we dine, the food is only one of the reasons for coming together. We gather together to enjoy each other's conversation, to share views and opinions, to reinforce relationships, and to celebrate what we have. The traditional Thanksgiving meal is a great example of this broader idea of dining.

Eating, on the other hand, is solely about the act of consuming food. It has little to do with a sense of a community or family. It's not surprising that we consume so much fast food—think of the term itself: Eat quickly and get on with more important things like shopping or watching television!

The distinction between dining and eating is important. When we give up on dining and just eat and run, we sacrifice a family ritual that has a real purpose. Family gatherings where genuine conversation takes place are the best way to deal with the issues that lead to clutter and disorganization in a home.

THINK IT THROUGH

Few surfaces in the home are greater magnets for clutter than the dining room or kitchen table. That beautiful, large, flat surface practically cries out for things to be left on it—wrapping paper, bills, the mail, yesterday's homework, and piles of "I'll get to it later" clutter.

My clients Melanie and Jane had not used their dining room table for two years. It was so covered in bills, toys, school projects, and junk mail that neither they nor their three children could remember what the surface looked like. When asked to imagine the vision they had for that room, they answered together that they wanted a place where the family could meet over meals, laugh, enjoy one another's company, and bond as a family. When they became inspired by the shared vision they had for their family and the dining room, they were ready to declutter the space and inspired to keep it organized and functional.

The dining room table should be considered sacred space in your home. It is a TV-free gathering place where the family has regular opportunity to talk about issues affecting them and to reiterate their visions for the life they want to live as individuals and as a family. I'm not saying you should sit down at the table and say, "Let's reiterate our visions," but when we talk to each other about what happened that day, or how we want to spend the weekend, or what annoyed us, we're creating that vision.

I recently worked with a family who had two children in their early teens. The girls had *never* eaten a meal at the dining room table because it was covered in paperwork and clutter. The family often ate on their back porch or with plates on their knees in front of the television. The daughters squealed with glee when they saw the transformation of their dining space. The main reason they were so enthusiastic? They said that they wanted to have a place where they could talk with their parents about their school days and where friends could join them for meals. Nothing should stand in the way of these desires.

SET IT UP

- Refer to your Room Function Chart and have everyone sign on.
- Establish zones for the different activities that take place in the dining room.
- Remove what *doesn't* belong in the room.

MAKE IT HAPPEN

Establish the zones

The purpose of the dining room is to have a pleasant place in which to enjoy your family while you share a meal. Keep the area not only free of cutter, but also off-bounds to the television and other distractions that stop you from interacting fully with one another. A clean, uncluttered dining area helps maintain calm and relaxation when you gather together. Remember: This is your dining zone—anything that doesn't contribute to that function should be removed from the space. Keep it simple and elegant. All you need in the dining area is a clear table for eating and storage space for dishes, formal china, and entertaining supplies.

Keep what you use close at hand

Take out all the plates and dishes that you use for meals and arrange them on your dining room table. Think about the way you use your dining room and the types of meals you have there. Do you need and use all of the flatware and glasses that you currently own? How many people use these items? How often do you entertain? Are they usually small, intimate gatherings or large family affairs?

Gather matching flatware and glasses together on the table. Discard any that you no longer like or use, as well as any that are chipped or damaged. As you return these items to a cupboard or hutch, place those that you use most frequently within easiest reach. Large serving platters and anything that you use less often should be placed on the lowest or highest shelves or toward the rear of the cupboard.

The table

The dining room table can end up the focus of family activity. Everything from crossword puzzles and model airplane building to homework and gift wrapping. Make it a rule to clear the area when each project is finished so that the table is always available to everyone and ready for mealtimes. No cheating. The table is always kept empty.

Formal china

If you have formal china, do you guard it as if it were a national treasure? China can be expensive and beautiful, but what's the point of owning it if you never use it? This is not to say that you should serve your three-year-old hot dogs on a Royal Copenhagen platter, but please try to use and enjoy it. And don't keep family china if it isn't meaningful to you.

Linens and napkins

If possible, it's a great idea to keep all of your table linens, tablecloths, and napkins in your dining room. Some people prefer to hang large tablecloths in a closet—whatever works best for you if you have the room.

Assign a drawer or shelf for linen sets so that anyone setting the table or putting things away can easily see where things belong. If you are short on space in the dining room, visit your local hardware store and purchase a shallow drawer than can be attached to the underside of the dining room table itself. Keep linens clean, dust free, and readily accessible.

REALITY CHECK—PROTECT YOUR INVESTMENT

To protect good china and flatware, invest in cloth storage sets that provide special protection for special-occasion china and stemware. These protectors zip closed and come with foam-padded dividers and foam separators for placement between each plate to avoid chipping and damage.

Bathroom

RECENT STATISTICS SUGGEST that you spend close to five years of your life in the bathroom. That's right—*five years!* (All the more reason to eat your fiber.) What better reason to make your bathroom the kind of place where you want to spend time. Most families have far more in their bathrooms than the room can reasonably accommodate. I had a client named Kurt who loved the lure of the bulk purchase stores and had a keen eye for a bargain. Whenever he saw toilet paper on sale, he would buy the largest package available. When I went to his house he had over 250 rolls of toilet paper. They filled every cupboard in the bathroom and most of the storage in the laundry. He laughed at how ridiculous it was, but just couldn't seem to help himself. We established one entire cupboard for toilet paper storage and Kurt agreed to give away most of the toilet paper to his friends and that going forward he would only buy toilet paper if it fit into that cupboard. My guess was that it'd be at least a year before he had to make another purchase!

Bathroom products are inexpensive and tempting. They smell so good! They make promises about changing your skin, your hair, your life. But it's very important to keep bathrooms clutter-free. Mold, mildew, germs, and grime love clutter—especially in a warm, damp space like a bathroom. It's close to impossible to keep it clean and hygienic if there's stuff everywhere.

THINK IT THROUGH

It's easy to accumulate products—your skin will be so soft; your hair will grow back, filling in that bald spot. Your lashes will be thicker and longer than ever! To keep your bathroom clean and clear, you're going to have to let go of those hopes and dreams, no matter how much you spent on them. You'll be surprised at how good a clean bathroom can be for your complexion!

SET IT UP

- Refer to your Room Function Chart and have everyone sign on.
- Establish zones for the different functions of the bathroom.
- Remove what *doesn't* belong in the room.

MAKE IT HAPPEN

Figure out the best zones

If the bathroom is shared, the zones can be dictated by person instead of by purpose. Give each family member a section of storage to use for him or herself. One sure way to improve traffic flow is to equip each person in the house with their own bathroom caddy. They can keep it either in a cupboard in the bathroom or in their room, taking it to the bathroom whenever they shower or bathe. This makes it easy for everyone to find exactly what they use. Plus, in a pinch, the finishing touches to your teenager's look can be completed somewhere other than the bathroom with you banging on the door trying to get in!

There will always be some shared products that are better organized by function. While prescription medications should be kept in individual areas, over-the-counter family medicines like flu and cold treatments and first-aid supplies should be centralized.

If competition isn't an issue in the bathroom, use clear plastic caddies or in-cupboard drawers to store like things together. Medicines in one area, hair care in another, cosmetics in a third. If you use certain items frequently, keep them in a top drawer or easily accessible cupboard. Keep extra supplies like soap, shaving cream, or toothpaste in an area away from the most heavily trafficked area in the bathroom. This will help you to see quickly what you have and avoid unnecessary purchases. It will also help you know when it's time to replace something.

Keep flat surfaces clear

It is impossible to keep any flat surface clean if it is cluttered with products and cleanliness is extremely important in the bathroom. Steam, moisture, and condensation promote mold and mildew. Add clutter and you have all the ingredients for an unhealthy and unsightly room. Keep your beauty products to a minimum so that you can quickly and easily wipe down countertops. It also helps to keep some cleaning products in a plastic caddy under the sink so that you have quick access to the sponges, sprays, and wipes you need to keep the room spotless.

Use vertical space

If you have trouble keeping flat surfaces clear in the bathroom, look to the available vertical space you have. Install hooks or towel rods on the back of the bathroom door to hang towels and robes.

Maximize your vertical space by purchasing an over-the-toilet cabinet or install shelves or cabinets that allow you to neatly store many of the items that live in the bathroom. Baskets, small containers, or trays are a great way to keep like things together. Put medications in one, hair products in another, first-aid materials in a third, and so on.

Shower caddies now come in many shapes and sizes. Some hang from the showerhead or are attached to a tension pole that fits into the corner of the shower. Invest in one that is sturdy, easy to clean, and large enough to hold the different shower products used by members of your family.

Purge unused products

If those miniature bottles of shampoo and conditioner you brought back from vacation last year have still not been used, they never will be. And that mango-papaya–scented foot lotion that was on sale last Thanksgiving at the drugstore? Time for it to go! Every six months, do a quick check on what's in the bathroom and get rid of all the bottles and tubes you haven't opened or used in that time. Every six months is also when you should replace your toothbrush. Instead of using cheap, harsh products to clean the bathroom, invest in high-quality items that smell great. Remember that less is more and you'll never have to look at that ugly black mold under the twenty-something product bottles in your shower again!

Cosmetics

All makeup has an expiration or use-by date. Sometimes it is stamped on the product itself, sometimes on the packaging. Regardless, most makeup goes bad in six months! A good rule of thumb, however, is that the closer the product is used to the eyes, the shorter the lifespan.

Mascaras go bad more quickly than everything else; they are good for about four months. Other cosmetics, lotions, and so on are generally good for about twelve months.

Perfume has a shelf life of three years. On some perfumes there is a manufacturer's code listed on the bottom of the bottle. This code might look something like AJ6546. The last number, in this case 6, indicates the year in which the perfume was made; it is most likely the perfume was manufactured in 2006. This particular bottle would be good until 2009.

It is always best to check with the manufacturer of the cosmetic if you are unsure of how to determine the use-by date of that product. Every cosmetic manufacturer has an 800 customer service number that can assist you.

Medications

All medications have an expiration date. Go through your medicine cabinet once a year to toss old drugs and treatments for problems you no longer have. All you have to remember in the bathroom is to keep it simple. You know perfectly well what products you no longer use. None of them are terribly expensive. Just toss them. It will become painless as you get used to it.

REALITY CHECK—CLUTTER AND HEALTH

Often people say that their homes aren't dirty, they're just cluttered. But clutter inhibits you from being able to clean your home well, as it's hard to clean behind and around things. Clutter promotes the buildup of dirt and allergens and increases your household's chances of respiratory problems. The health problems caused by clutter aren't just physical. In 1996, psychologists defined compulsive hoarding syndrome as a psychological disorder. In homes with severe cluttering, the residents nearly always suffer from anxiety or depression or both.

Garage, Basement, and Other Storerooms

KAY AND PAUL'S GARAGE looked like a cross between a storage facility and a car repair shop. There was a classic 1956 convertible taking up most of the room. The car was partially restored and most of the rest of the space in the garage was filled with spare parts, tools, paint, rims, tires, and car manuals. Apparently, Paul had bought the car soon after he started his first job and had been restoring it since then—fourteen years ago! Paul's family had owed a similar car when he was a child and for him the car had great memories of family vacations, weekend trips, and getaways. With a little prompting, Paul agreed that fourteen years was too long for any project and negotiated with his wife that unless he finished the restoration within six months the car would go. I have another client who had a box full of a hundred pounds of fake dirt she was storing in her garage for a friend who used it in an art installation. Fake dirt! Maybe that isn't your exact situation, but how much did your car cost? I'm guessing it's one of your most costly possessions. So why are you keeping it out on the street, exposed to the elements? Sun, rain, and snow do damage to your expensive car, yet your garage is protecting stuff that you likely seldom use. Does that make sense?

Garages are stuff cemeteries: Just because you have the space, doesn't mean you have to fill it. That said, the garage is one place where—even with the car comfortably parked therein—genuine storage can take place. Garages, basements, and storerooms are legitimate storage areas, but only if you're filling them with items that truly deserve to be stored, such as seasonal decorations and furniture, sports equipment, gardening or hobby tools, car supplies, and tools. The garage is a suitable place for these possessions even if they are things you actually use, and they are properly labeled and stored so that you can find them when you need them.

DEAR PETER:
I'm a stickler for details. I like everything to be clean and organized, but my husband is just the opposite. Our three-car garage is completely stuffed with the remains from his various projects—including a half-built canoe. I'm not kidding. A canoe. He's never been canoeing in his life.

THINK IT THROUGH

Garages and storage areas can be tough places to declutter and get organized. They are often one of the most serious problem areas in a home, in part because it's not even pretending to be a space where you try to live. It's a real storage space, so everything with no place in the house gets shoved in there. These are places where labels and bins really do solve problems. To get the job done, there are a few things you should keep in mind.

SET IT UP

- Refer to your Room Function Chart and have everyone sign on.
- Establish zones for the different functions of the garage and storage areas.
- Remove what *doesn't* belong in the room.

MAKE IT HAPPEN

Start slow

Let's assume we're working on your garage—although everything here equally applies to any storage area in your home. It's taken months or even years for your garage to become cluttered, so it may not be realistic to try and organize everything in one day or even a weekend. If this is the case for you, commit to starting small—one section of the garage at a time. Make a commitment every day to declutter and organize another section until it's done.

Streamline

Get rid of items you haven't used in over a year. If you haven't touched something in the last twelve months, chances are you are never going to use it. Do all those seasonal decorations actually get used? What about that sports equipment? Forget the excuses—now is the time to free up space by letting go of unused and unneeded items.

Get stuff off the floor

Once items start spreading across the floor, it's almost impossible to keep them under control. Use vertical space to increase your storage space and to avoid "floor creep"! Install a good, sturdy shelving system to store the items you decide to keep. Remember, though, that you only have the space you have. The volume of stuff, the number of boxes, or the size of storage containers is determined by the shelving space you have. Don't overload the garage just because you have the space!

Divide your garage into zones

Organize the items you keep in your garage into like groups—garden supplies, tools, camping supplies, sporting goods, bulk food storage, seasonal items, and so on. Use appropriate containers and labeling to identify specific items. Consider color coding different areas. An orange Peg-Board for tools, a green wall where the kids hang their bikes, blue hooks and bins for sporting gear. This will help everyone in the house see where things belong and encourage order from the chaos. Maintaining zones in your garage will also help avoid unnecessary purchases and assist in keeping things organized and tidy.

FYI—GARAGE AND BASEMENT SAFETY

Do not store highly flammable items like kerosene, paint thinner, or gasoline in your basement or garage unless they are in a tightly sealed container in a closed—and preferably locked—cupboard. Ensure that your basement and garage, like the rest of your home, are fitted with smoke detectors and keep a fire extinguisher handy. Keep a clear, clutter-free space of at least eighteen inches around your furnace to avoid a potential fire hazard.

Jump in at the deep end!

If you are a brave soul, once a year drag everything out of your garage. Get the whole family involved. Commit to getting rid of 50 percent of what is in the garage. Go through all boxes, bins, storage cupboards. Be brutal! If you aren't using an item—get rid of it.

Tools, paints, and chemicals

Where did that third hammer come from? Most of us will never need three hammers, so now is the time. Empty out your toolbox or cupboard and get rid of duplicates and tools you never use. Get rid of tools and materials you acquired for specific projects that are finished or will never get done. Throw away those ten thousand loose nails and screws, the Allen wrenches that come with the "assemble-it-yourself" furniture, and the curtain rod hardware you've been keeping even though you've thrown away the curtain rod.

Check all paint cans to see that the paint is still usable. As you open each can, label it with a number and paint a little patch on a piece of paper next to that number. Match the paints to the rooms in your home and create a paint guide that shows the number, the room, and the brand and code for the paint. Get rid of any paints that no longer match the rooms in your home. Check with your local city or town hall to find the best way to get rid of paints or other chemicals in a safe and environmentally friendly way.

Seasonal items

The neat thing about seasonal items (from a professional organizer's perspective anyway) is that every time you take them out or put them back away you have an opportunity to assess whether you really need to keep them. If you didn't use that glow-in-the-dark skeleton this Halloween, ask yourself if it's really worth storing away for another year. More than most things stored in a garage or basement, it's the seasonal decorations that often are a cause of tension. If you have the space and they're stored properly, that's great. If not—you know the drill!

Collections and mementos

Ask yourself if those items stored in a trash bag or old box in the garage are really that important to you. If they aren't honored and respected, maybe they are really clutter that you do not need to hold on to. If you truly treasure items, display them proudly and properly in your home.

Label, label, label

Garages and basements are often used for seasonal items, sporting equipment, holiday decorations, or medium- to longer-term storage. Be sure to clearly label any box, bin, or container that goes into the garage so that items can be easily and quickly located. Consider different colored labels for boxes or containers of like things—orange for Halloween decorations, white for holiday lights, green for unread books . . . stop right there! That was a trick! There should be no unread books in the garage!

Look to the stars

Consider using the ceiling of your garage for storage. Any hardware store carries a wide variety of hooks that can be used to hang bikes, sporting gear, or even gardening tools. Items like storm windows or summer window screens can easily be stored on ceiling rafters. Remember: You are creating useful storage, not space to hide away clutter you've removed from the rest of your house. All it takes is a little creativity to discover new storage solutions to old problems.

REALITY CHECK—HOLIDAYS

The Associated Press reported that for Christmas 2005, which fell on a Sunday, several megachurches canceled services. Why? Because it interrupts the gift giving. For many people in this country, Christmas is all about presents. Target stores now sell upside-down Christmas trees so you can have more room around the base for gifts. Sounds like a gimmick? Target has three variations on the upside-down tree, ranging in price from three hundred to five hundred dollars. Hammacher Schlemmer couldn't keep their six-hundred-dollar upside-down tree in stock!

Christmas isn't just about children; we also buy presents for extended family and colleagues and friends. It's so hard to perfectly understand someone else's taste. Many of the gifts we're given become the clutter in our garages and storage spaces. Here are a few ways to pull the reins in on holiday giving.

- If you have a large family, at Christmas draw names out of a hat. Next year, you're responsible for giving to the person you pick.
- If you have a large family, consider only giving gifts to the kids.
- Give disposable gifts or gifts that don't take up room (gift certificates, food baskets, charity donations, etc.) to business associates.
- Before you even start shopping, decide on a number of gifts that you're buying for your kids. Stop when you're done.
- Get your child one and only one big-ticket item like a bicycle or a dollhouse.
- Immediately donate to charity gifts that are age-inappropriate or duplicates of things you or your child already owns.

Step 4

Maintenance

THIS BOOK isn't about doing a big cleanup and returning to business as usual. Oh, if only it were that easy. If you've ever been on a fad diet, you know that starving yourself doesn't work. You might lose some weight, but as soon as you "finish" the diet, you gain all the weight back and more. The best diets aren't short-term fad diets. The weight stays off if you change your eating habits forever. The same goes for clutter. We're not talking about a clutter crash diet, we're talking about a lifestyle change. The good news is that maintaining a home that is clutter-free and relaxing is a whole lot easier than denying yourself ice cream and french fries. If you follow these maintenance guidelines, you'll never have to spend more than a few minutes here and there keeping your clutter under control.

ZONE MAINTENANCE

Maintenance begins when you've achieved your ideal. Your house is a place where you are relaxed and comfortable and inspired to live the life you want. You're surrounded with things that are meaningful to you. You remember the past, look forward to the future, but live in the present. You've found the right balance.

Now look around you. Everything has a home and everyone in the household knows where that home is. This may sound obvious to you, but some people aren't in the habit of assigning everything a spot, and chances are one of these people lives in your home! If a dish is out, they put it in a cabinet—wherever there's space. Sure, this is better than leaving it out on the counter, but it consumes space and time, space because you're not pairing like items together, and time because you won't know where to look when you next need that item.

So make sure everyone in your home knows and follows the golden rules: If you get it out—put it away. If you open it—close it. If you finish it—replace it. If it's full—empty it. If you take it off—hang it up. If it's dirty—wash it. If it's garbage—trash it.

ZONE SCAVENGER HUNT

Test your household's zone knowledge by playing a reverse kind of hide-and-seek. Everyone runs around the house and picks out three items (e.g., Grandma's gingham tablecloth, the sewing kit, unpaid bills, the Christmas wreath). Meet in a central spot, and write the items everyone has picked in a numbered list. Everyone writes his or her name on a piece of paper. Now, on your paper, write down the locations of the items in the numbered list. Whoever gets the most right wins. Whoever gets the least right has to put everything back in its proper place.

DAILY PURGING

You'd be amazed at how much you can accomplish in ten minutes. Every day, take five minutes to straighten up and five minutes to focus on cleaning out the clutter in a drawer or on a shelf or flat space, and your house will always be in order. Think about it—if you do this five days out of every week, you'll have purged 260 small areas in your home at the end of a year. Those small projects really add up.

It's best to use the same time slot every day. If you're a stay-at-home mom, do it when the kids nap or leave for school. If you're a morning person who either works from home or never has trouble getting to work on time, then make it part of your morning ritual. If you're always in a rush in the morning, pick a time when you get home—as soon as you walk in the door, or after dinner, or after the kids are in bed—whatever makes the most sense for you. One of my clients likes to straighten up in the morning so she comes home to a clean house. She saves her purge for the evening so that she can be sure to finish up. These small steps really make a difference!

THE FIVE-MINUTE PURGE

Here's what the five-minute purge looks like:
1. Set the kitchen timer for five minutes.
2. Grab a medium-size garbage bag. You'll use this bag to throw things away or to drop them off at your charity of choice, whichever makes more sense for the items you're purging.
3. Pick your target. Make sure to keep it small so you can be thorough. It's one drawer in the kitchen, one shelf of video tapes, the floor of the coat closet, etc.

4. Clear out anything you haven't used for the last six months to a year. Remember? You were supposed to have done this when you first cleaned your home. But a home is a living thing and what you felt you needed to keep yesterday, you may be able to let go of today. Now be ruthless. The more you get rid of, the longer you can wait before you revisit this area.

5. When the timer goes off, stop. If the bag is full, put it in the garbage (or in your car trunk so you can drop it off the next time you drive past a Goodwill or other charity). If the bag isn't full, put it with the garbage or recycling in preparation for tomorrow, when you'll surely fill it up in your next purge.

THE IN/OUT RULE

It's very simple. Now that your home is the way you want it, for everything that comes into your home, something must go. The thing that goes must either be the same type as the new item or take up the same amount of room. You buy a pair of shoes; you get rid of a pair of shoes. Easy enough, but it gets a little harder when we're talking about getting rid of your old TV, which still works perfectly well. The temptation is to keep it, even though you've got a huge, fancy, new TV. The new one can go in the den and you can just move the old one to the kitchen! Well, that's a major lifestyle decision. Do you want to watch TV in the kitchen, too? Is that part of your plan for the function of that room? When you plan to purchase a new, space-consuming item, part of the plan should be what you're going to get rid of to make room for the new purchase.

Did you know that there are millions of households in the United States who *never throw anything away*? You may not fall into this category, but as we all know, it's hard to part with stuff that cost hard-earned money. So, needless to say, the easiest way to follow this rule is to buy less. You need to control the inflow. When you go shopping, how do you separate what you want from what you need? Do you plan in advance? Do you know exactly what you're looking for when you're on your way to the store? Do you only buy what you planned to get? If you buy something that wasn't on your list or in the plan, ask yourself: Is this something I need or something I want? Do I have one already? What is my plan for the one I already have?

TIPS FOR CONTROLLING IN/OUT

For clothes/toys: Buy one, get rid of one.

Cost versus space: We usually take more time with expensive purchases. But remember, the more space something takes up, the more it costs you. Spend more time deciding to buy bigger items.

Time delay: Impose a time delay on every expenditure to curtail spontaneous purchases.

Find it, love it—wait forty-eight hours to purchase it.

Experience fund: Every time you stop yourself from making a spontaneous purchase, put the money that you would have spent in a special account called your "experience fund."

Pick an experience that your whole household can look forward to—a trip to Paris, the beach, Disneyland, etc. If your child asks for a toy at the store, you can do the same thing. Say, "This toy costs nine dollars and ninety-nine cents. Let's put that in the Disneyland fund instead." At the end of twelve months, I promise you'll have enough money to have an experience that the whole household will remember forever.

COMMUNICATION

Remember, different things are important to different people for different reasons. There are emotions attached to the work we're doing here. Take the time to understand one another. Make communicating about your home part of how you interact with your family. Get to a place where the cleaning-out process isn't accusatory or adversarial and you will find ways of decluttering that work for everyone.

RESOLVING CLEANUP CONFLICTS

Resolve conflicts, particularly when kids are involved, by divvying up responsibilities.

1. Have everyone keep track of the household chores they accomplish in a single week and the time they spent on each one. At the end of the week, compare charts.
2. Using the above exercise, redistribute chores to even out the time each person spends cleaning up and helping out. Create a job chart.
3. Your job chart can include:
   - Sorting mail
   - Doing laundry (kid-friendly)
   - Folding laundry (kid-friendly)

continued

- Taking out trash (kid-friendly)
- Paying bills
- Setting the table (kid-friendly)
- Doing the dishes (kid-friendly)
- Straightening your bedroom (kid-friendly)
- Walking the dog (older kid-friendly)
- Feeding pets (kid-friendly)
- Cleaning up after pets (kid-friendly)

KEEP A CHARITY BAG

Always, always, always have a garbage bag for charity donations. When you try on a piece of clothing and it doesn't look good on you, consider putting it in the bag. If you walk into your closet and see a picnic backpack that you've never used, put it in the bag. If you're given a gift you don't love, put it in the bag. When your youngest child outgrows an article of clothing, check it for stains; if it's in good shape, it goes straight in the bag. Make putting things in the charity bag a habit—the same way you throw away (or recycle) an empty food container.

When the bag is full, put it in your car. Depending on where you live, there's probably no need to plan a special trip to drop it off. Just keep it in the trunk until you're driving near your favorite charity. Get a receipt for tax purposes, and file it in your annual donations file (yes, you should have one).

DO THE MATH

I've said it a million times and I'll say it until I die: You need to do the math of value and cost. As soon as you calculate the *cost* of clutter, you'll realize that it's not worth holding on to things because of their *value*—because of what they're *worth*. Remember to think in terms of the life you want to live and the vision you have for your home.

Time costs
Does it take you longer than five minutes to tidy and clean up a room? If it takes longer, there's still too much clutter. How much time do you spend looking for your keys? Those minutes add up over a lifetime. Even if you only spend five minutes a day looking for lost items, that's thirty hours a year. More than a day. Now are you willing to take some time to clean up? Wouldn't you rather spend those five minutes calmly decluttering than running around in frantic frustration?

Space costs
No matter if you own or rent your space, you're paying per square foot. I'm not going to make you do the real math here, but when you lose your ability to enjoy a room or to store your expensive car in a proper garage, you're throwing that portion of your rent out the window. When you rent storage space you're wasting money, not solving the problem. When you move to a bigger home (or just fantasize about it) because you can't throw things away, you're throwing good money after bad.

REAP THE BENEFITS

There's no point to putting all this effort into reading this book, much less cleaning up your space, if you're not going to enjoy and take advantage of the change.

Emotional benefits
When your space is neat, clear, and free from clutter, you'll notice a change in the way you feel about your life and your rela-

tionships. Your rooms fulfill the functions you've chosen for them. Gathering places are comfortable for friends and family. Your bedroom is a romantic oasis. Enjoy the peace, pride, and satisfaction that come with living the life that you've chosen for yourself.

Financial benefits

When you organize your papers, your financial life improves. You can work toward paying off debt. Bills are paid on time. Not only that, when you start looking at all the stuff you own but don't use or appreciate, it should help you buy fewer items and spend less money. When you spend less time shopping, you spend more time finding new interests, being active in the outdoors, being with your family and friends.

Time benefits

Gone are the minutes and hours spent cursing yourself or blaming the dog for eating your homework. When everything has a place, getting ready in the morning takes less time. You won't be late. You won't forget important dates or arrive at a meeting without critical papers. Tax time is a breeze (except for the check-writing part). You will feel more relaxed, confident, and in control. Your time belongs to you, not your stuff.

Space benefits

The less clutter you have in your house, the more you can reap the benefits of free space. Now your family can sit down at the dining room table and enjoy a meal together. Now your family room is a comfortable place to relax. Now you can have friends over or host a spontaneous party. Gone is the shame and embarrassment of having a home that bears no resemblance to the person you want to present to the world. Revel in your space. Host parties. Show off! You've earned it.

Step 5

Cleanup Checkup

DECLUTTERING AND GETTING ORGANIZED takes commitment, focus, and, initially, a significant time commitment. By now you should be seeing some major changes in your home, your sense of well-being, and your attitude toward the things you have decided to keep. You know if you're winning the battle—you see the clear surfaces, feel the open space, have new, efficient routines, and experience the sense that anything is possible.

Either that, or you're still stuck in place, overly attached to stuff that doesn't bring you happiness, and deluding yourself about how much change you've actually made. Just how well did you do? Go back to the Clutter Quiz on page 22 to find out just how uncluttered your life is.

HOUSEHOLD SUMMIT

Now it's time to meet with your family and discuss what you did and didn't achieve. Create a forum for discussing important issues. Did compromises solve the problems? Are you able to use each room in your house for its intended purpose? Is your partner happy with your shared living space? Are your kids more relaxed and focused? Are you proud of your space? Is the anxiety about clutter gone? Is there a harmonious relationship between your home and the life you want to live in it?

Ask your children specific questions about whether their reorganized spaces work for them. Is it easier to find your toys? Do your homework? Do you enjoy working at your arts table or is it still too hard to fit the paper on it? Do you put your things away when you're finished with them? Is it okay to watch DVDs in the family room instead of Mom and Dad's room? Do you like eating in the dining room with the whole family? Is there anything else that would make your space more enjoyable for you?

Ask your partner bigger questions about life. Does he feel relaxed now when he gets into bed? Does he feel there is a sense of balance and calm in your home? Does she feel clear about what you both hope to gain from the lives you are living? Is there anything she thinks you could change at home to bring it closer to the life you both imagine?

Turn back to Step 2 (see page 80) and take out your Room Function Chart. Does each room do what you want it to do? Tour the zones. Is everything in the zone serving its purpose? Revisit the Questions for General Discussion on page 82. What is everyone committed to and are they sticking to their commitments?

RELAPSING

You've done it. Are you pleased with the new space in your home? Do you feel less overwhelmed? Do you rise in the morning ready to greet the day, your job, your family, your life, the challenges and opportunities that life has to offer? Is there room in your life for adventure and relaxation? I hope so.

Just because you've decluttered doesn't mean you're done. Vigilance is key. Clutter creeps back in. If you stay on top of it, you'll never have to open this book again. The next chapter shows you how you can keep the clutter at bay, around the calendar, for good.

Step 6

New Rituals

WHO WANTS TO SACRIFICE a whole Saturday to cleaning up the mess that your house has become? Who wants to spend the day before you host a party straightening up when you should be prepping food or getting a manicure? After all the effort you've just made, do you really want everything to slip back to the way it was? Because it can and will. With our culture of consuming—with all the junk mail and cheap clothes and short-lived trends—if you don't control your clutter, it will control you. If you've gone to all the trouble to follow the steps in this book, your house is now clutter-free. Let's keep it that way.

The secret to staying organized and maintaining a clutter-free home is to make organization a natural part of your life. I've talked about daily rituals throughout this book. Everything has a place. When you use something, put it away. After you wear something, return it to the closet or put it in the laundry. When you open a letter that requires action, discard the used envelope and put the letter into the mail tray. These small steps all help to create the home and the life that you want.

Keeping your home clutter-free takes more than small

steps. Things fall into disrepair. New hobbies fall by the way-
side. You outgrow clothes. Stuff accumulates. Even the best in-
tentions can get sidetracked, and your weekly bag-in-hand
clutter control may have slipped a bit. The best way to manage
the never-ending clutter creep is to establish an annual cycle of
organization.

BEYOND SPRING CLEANING

We all know that spring has traditionally been a time of cleaning—after a long winter, the home was aired and every corner
was scrubbed clean. This ritual dates back to Old English times.
Well, times have changed. Before the industrial age, people had
less and homes were smaller. Clutter was not an epidemic.
Spring cleaning is still a great tradition, but it's time for a new,
year-round set of traditions that will help keep your home organized and clutter free.

THE CALENDAR FOR AN ORGANIZED HOME

January Fresh Start	*February* Shred Mania	*March* Reinvent Spring Cleaning
April Explore the Black Hole	*May* Discover the Great Outdoors	*June* Teach Your Children Well
July Have a Yard Sale	*August* Prepare for Back-to-School	*September* Make the Season Switch
October Brace Yourself for Winter	*November* Gear Up for the Holidays	*December* Relax and Enjoy

JANUARY—START FRESH

A new year. A new you! With the turning of the year, we all think about resolutions and what we can do better in the next twelve months. Make your resolutions realistic, write them down, and, most important of all, remember that a more organized life is a happier, less stressed life.

The holidays are a busy time. Why? Everyone's shopping. When you're busy, things tend to slip around the house. Bills fall behind. And with all that shopping, more stuff sneaks into your home. Start the year right by taking control of postholiday clutter.

Purge the holiday decorations

When you take down your decorations—whether it's the lights on the house or the ornaments on the tree—it's a great time to discard old, unused, or broken decorations. Also limit decorations to the space you have, and clearly label the boxes in which they are stored. Use different boxes for each holiday to avoid confusion and help keep order. A little effort here will pay off next holiday season!

Use the right storage containers

Using divided boxes for tree ornaments and flat, sectioned boxes for wreaths will ensure that expensive items are not crushed or damaged in storage. Large, plastic stackable bins are great for lights, decorations, and larger seasonal items. Label them clearly and store them in the less-trafficked zone of your home or garage. Consider numbering bins and creating a master list of what each contains. Here's a bin label sample:

Bin number:	
Season:	
Stored in:	
Contents:	

Print out a stack of these labels and attach one to the front of each bin so that you can clearly and quickly find what you're looking for.

Holiday In/Out

Remember the In/Out Rule—you don't want more to come in than goes out. But holidays tend to be one-way. Items come in, in, in! What goes out? Now's the time to examine your haul and see what items of equivalent size and use can go. Did you get a new sweater? Time to toss an old one. Donate old versions of new electronics. Don't go from being a two-TV family to a three-TV family just because you were given a new one. By the time you die, every single room will have its own TV. Who needs that?

When you give, be sensitive to the clutter issues your friends and family may have. Make it a policy to always give a gift receipt. That way it can be exchanged for something the giftee really wants or needs.

FEBRUARY—SHRED MANIA

All my clients complain that paperwork gets on top of them at some point. It's inevitable. But if you make a concerted effort to clean shop once a year, you can keep the paperwork under control.

Get a jump on your tax return

Prepare your taxes and file as early as you can to ensure a quick refund. Discard and shred financial records and other documentation that you no longer need to back up your returns. Label and file current tax records.

Now is the time to go through important papers, files, and documents. Go through your files and throw out old files or paperwork that you no longer need or use. You'll find that papers that seemed important six months ago are irrelevant now. Perhaps a few months of unnecessary utility bills have crept into your files. Refer to Tax Stuff on page 151 to remind yourself of what you should be keeping. Update any insurance policies or legal documents, such as wills, as needed. Make a photocopy of any new policies, credit cards, or other critical documents acquired in the last twelve months and store the copies in a secure location. Once you've made sure that everything is up to date and accurate, give that shredder a workout.

Create a message center

Designate a specific area in your home to post announcements or invitations, a family calendar, and messages. You can hang your keys and keep your loose change in this area, too. Mail should be processed right nearby. Maintain and update a list of frequently used telephone numbers in this area, as well as emergency contacts and any other information that might be needed at a moment's notice. Divide the board into areas for each family member so that everyone knows where to post a note or message for someone specific.

MARCH—REINVENT SPRING CLEANING

We all know about spring cleaning—in theory. Here's how to put it into practice in today's world. These tasks will leave your home sparkling, inside and out.

SPRING CLEANING TASK LIST	PERSON RESPONSIBLE	MATERIALS NEEDED
INSIDE:		
Clean windows.		
Dust and clean tops of cabinets and electric appliances.		
Steam-clean carpets.		
Launder winter bedding and blankets before storing.		
KITCHEN:		
Deep clean all appliances inside and out.		
Clean behind and under refrigerator.		
Thoroughly clean inside cupboards and refrigerator.		
Discard outdated food items from your pantry and freezer.		
Organize like items together around the "magic triangle."		
Discard pots, pans, and utensils that are seldom or never used.		
Clear all flat surfaces.		
Restock kitchen cleaning caddy.		
Thoroughly clean the black hole under the sink!		continued

SPRING CLEANING TASK LIST	PERSON RESPONSIBLE	MATERIALS NEEDED
CLOTHES:		
Discard clothes that you no longer love, wear, or look great in. Donate unwanted items to your favorite charity.		
Arrange like items together in your closet.		
Color coordinate your clothing so that you can clearly and easily see what is in your wardrobe.		
Store away winter clothes.		
Replenish cedar blocks or mothballs to protect from moths and insects.		
OUTSIDE:		
Remove storm windows, make sure they're labeled, and then store carefully to avoid damage.		
Clean outside of windows.		
Store your snow-moving equipment.		
Do a quick maintenance check on your lawnmower and other gardening equipment. Reseed and fertilize your lawn.		
Check your garden hoses and breathe the first scents of spring.		

Make a schedule

Revise the above list to suit your particular needs. List all of the spring cleaning tasks inside and outside the house that need doing. Assign responsibilities to each family member and post the list on the fridge or in some central location so everyone can check progress.

Save the list so you can use it next year.

THE TEN-MINUTE GRAB BAG

Brainstorm with your family to come up with any organizing or decluttering task that can be completed in ten minutes or less—put toys away, organize one drawer in the kitchen, arrange T-shirts neatly, find old magazines and put them into the recycle bin—anything at all. List these tasks on small cards and place them into the "ten-minute box." Every night before dinner for one month, everyone grabs one card and completes the task. Lots of small steps will make a huge difference in thirty days.

Clean house party

Have a family celebration—a special meal, outing, or day trip— to mark the beginning of spring and the completion of spring cleaning. Let everyone celebrate their role in decluttering and organizing the house at the end of winter.

APRIL—EXPLORE THE BLACK HOLE

Whether it's the garage, that space under the stairs, the basement, the spare bedroom, or the attic, everyone has a favorite black hole for things that they don't need right away, might need someday, or just can't get rid of. It's time to tackle your storage areas!

Divide and conquer

Divide your home into four areas and tackle any storage closets in one zone each week during this month. The four areas might be the basement, bedrooms, living areas, and laundry—choose areas that make sense to you.

Spread the load

Ask friends or family to help if the amount of stuff in storage is large. This can help make the task manageable. Volunteer to return the favor.

Remember—you only have the space you have!

Cull the items you have stored to fit the space you have. Specify areas in your home for needed temporary storage—yard sale items, gifts for regifting, or borrowed items like books or videos that need to be returned.

Storage areas

Discard items no longer needed or used, store like items together, and clearly label storage containers and boxes. Remember that basements are often cold and damp while attics are prone to extreme temperatures. Check to make sure your stored items are surviving the elements. If you have a rented storage space, keep in mind that storage outside your home should only be used in extreme circumstances, and then only for a short period of time. Off-site storage is expensive and, like the old saying, out of sight is out of mind. Now's the time to reconsider your off-site storage space. How long have you had it? What if you take the plunge and sell or discard everything in there? Would your life change in any way (other than that you'd have one less bill to pay)?

MAY—DISCOVER THE GREAT OUTDOORS

A clutter-free and organized home frees you from stress and enables you to spend more time doing the things you want to do. Spending time outside your house is harder than just hanging around at home.

It requires initiative, planning, and energy. But the rewards are great—it's not like you're going to build a lifetime of memories by sitting in front of the TV. Take some time this month to focus on spending time outside of your house.

Prepare for the great outdoors

Check and fix outdoor play equipment: swings, slides, bikes, etc. Fire up the grill to make sure it's in working order. Hose off outdoor furniture and (if you're lucky enough to have one) make sure your pool equipment is in working order for those long, hot days ahead. Be realistic about which outdoor stuff you do and don't use. That picnic backpack someone gave you as a wedding gift? It may be stylish, but if you haven't used it yet, it's time for it to go. What about the bikes, Rollerblades, or the basketball hoop you never put up? These are big items that take up lots of space. If they're only fantasies, now's the time to enact the fantasy or ditch the item.

Plan a summer vacation

Now's the time to use all that money you made at yard sales or saved by not buying things you didn't need. Gather the whole family together to talk about summer possibilities and plans. Involve everyone in the planning and decision making. Divide tasks so that everyone has a role to play in organizing the family vacation.

Organize kids' summer activities

Work with your kids to schedule their summer vacation activities. A simple weekly chart of what's happening can create a great deal of enthusiasm and help you plan ahead. Involve other families in the neighborhood to share the load. If you plan day trips to the pool, beach, or museums in advance, schedule play dates and picnics, and create anticipation for any family trips or camp, then your kids will have a clear sense of how the summer will pass. This sense of order is both reassuring and exciting— and very helpful when it comes time for that "How I Spent My Summer Vacation" back-to-school essay.

JUNE—TEACH YOUR CHILDREN WELL

"But Mom, I'm bored!" Nobody wants to hear that all summer. Now's the time to get your children involved in the maintenance of good systems in your home. Reward their positive behavior and let them see that decluttering and organization have definite benefits.

Tackle your kids' spaces

Work with your children to identify what is working and what's not in their bedrooms. Make a project of their personal space. Identify as many zones as make sense for your child—reading, clothes, homework, crafts, computer games, laundry. Have fun making artistic labels for the areas. Work with your child to make sure that items are in their correct area.

Make kid-friendly closets

Our closets need change as we age, so make sure your child's closet suits him or her. Are her favorite things easily accessible? Make room by putting off-season items high up on shelves, get everything but shoes off the floor, and buy or build appropriate storage containers for the things she needs every day. Help your child decide which clothes and shoes it's time to discard. Before you know it, you'll have a clean closet.

Tackle the toys

Gather old toys, games, and books that are no longer used or age-appropriate. Even consider establishing a giveaway bin or a broken-toy bin so your child can make these decisions part of regular cleanup. When you go to make the charity drop-off, bring your children along. That way they can make the donation themselves and learn the value of giving to others less fortunate than themselves.

Limits and routines

Your child's toy, book, and clothing limits should be clearly set by the size of the toy containers, bookshelves, and dresser or closet. Reinforce these agreed-upon limits. Make it part of your household routine to identify items that need to be donated to charity or sold at a yard sale. Without the pressure of school, create or revise a schedule of chores. Make sure you and your child agree that it will still work when school starts again and homework becomes a factor.

Rewards

No child is going to enjoy sitting around organizing his room all summer. Make the projects as fun as you can. Find a balance between organization and play. Spread projects out throughout the summer. It never hurts to schedule less-than-thrilling tasks next to favorite activities. For example, you might go to the pool every Saturday after addressing one of the zones in your child's room. And remember to keep everything on a calendar which you and your child discuss and anticipate.

JULY—HAVE A YARD SALE

The middle of summer is a great time to purge, and the long days are perfect for a yard sale. Don't have a yard? You're not off the hook. Those warm nights can be great for tackling your clutter digitally.

Go online and make a dollar

Consider using an online auction site to get the best price for items you are looking to sell. Not everything sells well online, but sporting goods, electronics, brand-name clothes, jewelry, collectibles, and automotive parts are some of the items that generally return great prices. If you're a registered eBay user, you can look up completed sales for items similar to yours to see if they actually sold and at what price. No point in posting your item and paying the listing fees if there's no demand for your "treasure." If you're not tech-savvy or don't have the time to deal with posting the item, corresponding with the buyer, packing it up, and sending it, remember that you can use an eBay trading assistant if there's one in your area. You'll pay a commission, but it's all free money as far as I'm concerned.

The neighborhood yard sale

Lots of items don't lend themselves to online sales. Heavy furniture that requires crating or large, awkward, inexpensive items like bulletin boards can be more trouble than they're worth if you're not experienced with shipping. For all those items you don't want to sell online, organize the First Annual Neighborhood Yard Sale (see page 71 for details on how to organize a yard sale). If you and your neighbors organize together, you'll draw a bigger crowd and make better profits. Not only is this a great way to declutter, but you get to meet your neighbors and have a fun social day at the same time. Your kids can sell their used toys or set up a lemonade stand. But don't fall victim to your own scheme: No buying your neighbor's junk! And remember—whatever doesn't sell goes straight to charity or the trash! Make sure you've factored that into the schedule.

AUGUST—PREPARE FOR BACK-TO-SCHOOL

Once school starts up again, chaos descends. The pace in any household dramatically increases and it can be hard to keep up. Some good planning and a little organization can smooth the reentry into the school year and make your life that much easier!

Clothes and gear

Check your child's school clothing to make sure they have not outgrown it. Make sure your child has a sensible backpack and wet weather gear. For younger kids, purchase and hang a five-pocket clothing bag so that a week of clothes can be laid out in advance.

Home office and school supplies

Make sure your home office is fully stocked and check your children's school supplies. Decide where you can consolidate their craft or homework supplies and your office stuff so you can avoid duplication and unnecessary purchases. Organize the items so they are easy to locate and easy to replenish.

Digital cleanup

If your house is looking pretty clutter-free, set aside a few hours on a slow night to declutter and organize your computer files and digital assets. Delete old files; archive important files that are no longer active; delete poor-quality photos; post favorite photos to online sharing sites, or save them to CDs and send them out to family and friends. Download and install a desktop search tool like MSN Search's Windows Desktop Search to help you easily find items anywhere on your computer, including e-mails and attachments, in the same way a search engine searches the Web for you.

Shopping for school

Ask your children to draw up a list of what they think they need for the new school year, then check it together against what they already have. Use the resulting list as a basis for planning a shopping day. Consider giving them a budget and letting them make some purchases.

SEPTEMBER—MAKE THE SEASON SWITCH

As winter approaches, it's time to open up space in your closets for those bulky sweaters and to make sure that your summer items are properly stored out of the way.

Make space in your closets

Use a closet in the guest bedroom or another suitable space in the basement or attic to store your off-season clothes. Make sure the storage location is cool and dry and that all stored clothes are clean. Mothballs or cedar blocks will help keep moths and other pests at bay.

Discard what you no longer wear

Every time you switch clothes for the season, you should give your closet a quick once-over. If you didn't wear it this summer, are you really going to store it all winter only not to wear it next summer? Get rid of it. Also discard summer clothes that are torn, soiled, or just out of fashion.

OCTOBER—BRACE YOURSELF FOR WINTER

Those falling leaves are a sign that winter is around the corner, but don't go into hibernation mode yet. Better to clean out your garage and winterize your home before the first frost.

Garage cleanup

Your car is one of your most expensive and useful possessions. The goal here is to park it in the garage so the winter elements don't diminish your investment. Take everything out of the garage, sweep out dust and debris, and hose down the floor. Discard unused items, arrange like items together. If you haven't already, now's the time to install sturdy shelving to clear items off the floor.

Designate zones

Specify where items belong. Install shelving, a Peg-Board, and racks for sporting goods, tools, and storage bins. Label everything clearly. You can even mark areas on the floor for the kids' bikes. If the garage is a tight fit for your car, install mirrors to make parking easier. Check each zone to make sure it is meeting your storage needs.

Winterize the house

Clear gutters of leaves and debris. Have your chimney, fireplace, and furnace inspected. Make sure all your gardening tools and equipment are properly cleaned and stored out of the weather. Clean and install storm windows. Check doors and windows for drafts and reseal accordingly.

NOVEMBER—GEAR UP FOR THE HOLIDAYS

The holidays are supposed to be fun, right? So why spend hours looking for parking in the mall parking lot only to rush around grabbing last-minute gifts that you only half believe your family and friends will like? The secret to really feeling the holiday spirit is great organization. A little advance planning will keep you focused on family and celebration—not stress and discord!

Entertaining
Prepare for any meals and events you may be hosting using the planner on the following page.

Holiday card and gift lists
Consider using a PDA or a computer to electronically store names and addresses. This will enable you to quickly and easily print name and address labels for your holiday cards. It's also an efficient way to immediately save the addresses on the envelopes of cards you receive.

Take notes
Pay attention—you'll be surprised at how often family and friends mention items they're hoping or planning to buy or that you see an item you know one of them would love. Keep a list with the gift idea, the person it's for, and the date you had the idea on a page at the back of your daily planner. When it comes time to shop, the list will jog your memory. If it's been several months, you might want to check with someone in the know to make sure your recipient hasn't already bought or received the item.

Consider giving an "experience" rather than a "thing"
A concert, theater ticket, restaurant gift certificate, or even a donation to a particular charity can leave a more lasting impression than another bottle of perfume or unnecessary article of clothing.

DONE	TASK	PERSON RESPONSIBLE	MATERIALS NEEDED	RENTED	BORROWED OR PURCHASED?	PREP DAY
	Final guest list (see attached)					
Serving Dishes						
	Cups					
	Plates					
	Utensils					
	Serving platters					
	Serving utensils					
	Napkins					
	Pitchers					
	Punch bowls					
Food						
	Chips & dip					
	Brownies					
	Salads					
	Pigs in a blanket					
	Nuts & candy					
	Cheese & crackers					
	Ham					
	Garnishes					

DONE	TASK	PERSON RESPONSIBLE	MATERIALS NEEDED	RENTED	BORROWED OR PURCHASED?	PREP DAY
Beverages						
	Ice					
	Beer					
	Wine					
	Soda					
Party Favors						
Decorations						
	Balloons					
	Candles					

Keep the gift-giving under control

It's nice to be generous, but don't go overboard. There are lots of ways to exercise restraint when it comes to giving gifts, particularly if you have a large family or gift-heavy social circle. Gifts comprise a large chunk of clutter because they tend to be items with value that aren't exactly what you want or need. Suggest that the family or group set a price limit on gifts, use a family lottery to choose one person only to buy for, or purchase gifts only for the kids.

Go digital and save some legwork

Shop online—it's easy, fast, and shipping is often free around the holidays. If you're traveling, have gifts shipped directly to your destination. But make sure the recipient will be home to accept them, and make sure they don't get opened before you arrive! You can also buy groceries and other holiday purchases (even trees!) online. Save yourself a shopping trip, and spare yourself those impulse purchases that tend to go hand in hand with holiday shopping.

DECEMBER—RELAX AND ENJOY

As the rush and celebration of this month descend, let your vision for the life you want to live dance in your head (alongside the vision of sugarplums). The year is drawing to a close. Stop, take a moment to yourself, and reflect upon the past year.

Celebrate your successes

Enjoy the season, enjoy your family, and enjoy yourself! We seldom make time to reflect on our dreams or our achievements. Set aside time to think how you've tried to live a simpler, richer life with less junk. Be happy about your successes, be clear about where you feel you failed, and be realistic about what you can achieve in the new year.

Commit to making the changes you want

The number one New Year's resolution in America is to lose weight. For the coming year, why not consider shedding the extra weight of clutter that fills your home and bogs down your life. Commit to removing two garbage bags of items a day from your home—one of trash and one of items you're donating to charity—until the clutter is under control.

There's no way around it: Clutter doesn't clear itself. Staying ahead of it takes time and effort. I'm not a magician, but I *can* promise you that if you create new traditions, the clutter will never get out of control, and the words "It's all too much!" will never cross your lips again.

Afterword

Take What You've Learned into the World

At least once a week I am asked why I do what I do. People say, "Aren't all of those people slobs?" or "Won't they just fill their homes with clutter again ten minutes after you leave?" or, most frequently, "Why don't they just clean up their own mess?" It's enough of a pain to organize one's own life, why would I want to wade through other people's stuff?

This is a great question we should all ask ourselves at various points in our lives: Why do I do what I do?

A couple years ago I received an e-mail from a man in Arizona who had watched me work on *Clean Sweep* and wondered if I could possibly help him. Max had been married for twenty-five years and had two children who were in their early twenties. Four years earlier, his wife had been diagnosed with a brain tumor and after extensive surgery and radical chemotherapy had returned home. Unfortunately, the person who returned to the family home was radically different from the woman Max had married and the mother his children had known all their lives. She had become very unpredictable, antisocial, and developed an intense need to hold on to everything—clothing, mail, magazines, newspapers, even empty food containers, jars, and tins. Any attempt to remove the clutter made her very agitated, sometimes hysterical. It was not worth upsetting her so much and so the clutter grew and grew.

Throughout this time, Max's daughter became increasingly despondent and was diagnosed with severe depression. As time passed, Max's wife's condition slowly deteriorated and she returned to the hospital frequently. When Max e-mailed me, it had been three months since his wife had passed away. Two weeks after the funeral, Max's daughter took her own life.

Here was a man who was not quite fifty and had suffered horrendous loss. His son was away at college and he was alone in a house containing the clutter his ill wife had clung to so dearly. He hadn't entered his daughter's bedroom since her death. His deep grief was mingled with such an embarrassment at the state of the house that he couldn't bring himself to ask anyone he knew for help.

Max asked if I could come to Arizona and help him deal with belongings that filled the family home. I did so using many of the decluttering and organization techniques that are in this book. Of course, Max's situation was unique, but the power that the things in that home had over him, the crushing impact of memories, and the sense that he could not tackle this job alone are common to every home I enter.

Max and I worked together for three days to clear the clutter from his home. We dealt with his wife's and daughter's belongings in a way that honored and treasured their memories, but acknowledged that they were gone forever. At the end of our time together, the transformation in Max was astounding. It was as if a massive burden had been lifted from him. Was he still grief-stricken? Certainly. But was he better prepared to deal with the issues facing him and to move ahead in a healthy and balanced way? I honestly think so. The last thing that Max said to me as I left for Los Angeles was, "Thank you—this experience has freed me from so much and really changed my life."

Why do I do what I do? Because those three days were among the most enriching, memorable, and inspiring times of my life.

IT'S NOT ABOUT THE STUFF

My job may be all about organization and decluttering, but I cannot say enough times that it is not about "the stuff." I have been in more cluttered homes than I can count, and the one factor I see in every single situation is people whose lives hinge on what they own instead of who they are. These people have lost their way. They no longer own their stuff—their stuff owns them. I am convinced that this is more the norm than the exception in this country. At some point, we started to believe that the more we own, the better off we are. In times past and in other cultures, people believe that one of the worst things that can happen is for someone to be possessed, to have a demon exercise power over you. Isn't that what being inundated with possessions is—being possessed?

This is why I don't care that much about "the stuff." The stuff is secondary to what interests me, what challenges me, what drives me to do what I do. What I see every day are people who have lost their way in their own homes. Who are buried— literally and metaphorically—by what they own. You have no chance of being who you want to be, your best self, unless you dig out from under the weight of your clutter.

Getting organized for the sake of getting organized is a waste of time. Getting organized because it helps you live a richer, less stressed, happier, and more focused life, now that's a goal worth pursuing. If you are not organized or if you are struggling with clutter, you are spending too much time just getting through the day. You are not thriving, just surviving. Every single person I have worked with has had a moment of blinding insight where they suddenly redefine their relationship to what they own. No permanent change can happen without this shift.

You only have one life to live. How you live that life is your choice. As far as I know, no one has ever had "I wish I had bought more stuff" inscribed on their tombstone. What you own can easily blind you to who you are and what you can be. What I do and what I invite you to do is not just about organizing your closets or your garage or your sock drawer. It's about you and the life you can live. Declutter, get organized, and watch a whole world you hadn't noticed open up before you. It's been two years since Max's wife died. Last I heard from him he'd hiked part of the Appalachian Trail. I can't think of a better example of how, even faced with the most heartbreaking circumstances, you can always discover new dimensions to your life.

> DEAR PETER:
> I shared some of our experiences with my cousin and my dear friend on the phone last night, and they both made comments on the way I sounded on the phone. My voice was lighter and there was a smile in it somewhere, and I have to attribute it to the way you made me feel yesterday. As the MasterCard commercials say, many things can be bought, but true feelings and emotions are priceless. I feel empowered to clean up not only the mess in the garage, but in all of the other aspects of my life.

YOU CAN DO ANYTHING

If you are like most of the people I have worked with, your physical stuff has, at one time or another, cluttered not only your

home, but also your mind and your life. If you've truly followed
the steps in this book, you should now be free from that burden.
Once that weight has lifted, you have the opportunity to take
what you have learned in decluttering and organizing your
home and apply those principles to almost every aspect of your
life: your mind, your body, your career, your friendships, family,
and romantic relationships. You have an infinite capacity to
achieve greatness. I know it. I have seen it.

Declutter your health

You cannot expect to be healthy living in a house full of clutter.
Clutter has a great impact on your confidence and your mood.
Your home, your nest, is out of control. Rooms don't serve their
purposes. You're overwhelmed. Your values and priorities are
out of whack. All that clutter feeds a sense of low self-worth and
helplessness, which leads to less motivation to change. You're
caught in an unhealthy downward spiral.

Many of my clients who are struggling with clutter are also
struggling with anxiety and depression. Often they're on med-
ication. Research says that people who live with a high level of
clutter are more likely to experience:

- headaches,
- asthma, coughing, and other respiratory problems,
- sleeping problems,
- allergies,
- fatigue and low motivation.

Medications are often not effective because the problems are
endemic to the situation—mold, dust, dirt, and mildew grow
and thrive amid the clutter. The moment I move or disturb
any clutter, I can see millions of particles of dust and dirt re-
leased into the air—clutter seriously affects the air quality in
your home. This situation is hugely compounded when pets are

living in cluttered homes. And no surprise, cockroaches and other pests love clutter. They tend to hide and breed well in it.

Clutter also presents a physical danger. In Washington State, a woman was recently found dead, buried by piles of clutter in her home when they collapsed on top of her and suffocated her. Even if your clutter isn't a suffocation hazard, it's a fire hazard. Think about how snugly you pack newspapers and wood to build a nice, romantic fire in the fireplace. A cluttered home is a tinderbox. Now that you've gotten rid of your clutter, you've made your home a safer refuge.

Declutter your relationships

One thing that has shocked me in the course of my work has been how often I've seen relationships fall apart as their clutter is removed. In decluttering their homes, these people realize that the fear that motivated them to hold on to useless things has also blinded them to the real problems in their relationship. This may sound paradoxical—why would you want to clean up your life if it's going to destroy your relationship? Clutter never preserves a healthy relationship, and its removal won't destroy a fulfilling relationship. The only couples who break up in the face of a bright, clean, organized home are the ones who realize how much more they want and deserve from life.

The good news is this also works the other way. Couples who have been bogged down by their clutter can experience a revitalization of romance when their space and minds are cleared. The great thing about decluttering and getting organized is that it cannot be done without honesty and communication. Very quickly, couples find themselves talking openly about what they value, what they fear, and what is most important to them. For those whose relationship is based on what they own, or whose only sense of unity comes from the clutter, this process can be difficult and heartbreaking. But if your relationship has a strong base, the process of rethinking the function of your home and

your relationship to your belongings inevitably strengthens
what you have.

I've asked you to imagine the life you want and to use that vision in deciding what you keep and what you let go. Part of
imagining that ideal life is envisioning the relationship you
want—the companionship, the support, the love. If your life is
full of emotional clutter, now is the time to clear it away and to
look honestly at what you have and what you want.

Declutter your waistline

We have a weight problem in this country and it is killing us.
Two out of every three Americans are overweight and one third
of us are obese. In the space of a generation, we have become a
nation of fat people and our children are right there with us. It's
no coincidence that at the same time our waistlines are expanding, the problem with clutter in our homes is becoming so wide-
spread. The two are intimately connected.

We have become a nation of out-of-control consumers—we
spend too much, we buy too much, and we eat too much. In the
same way that we surround ourselves with so much clutter, we
overwhelm our bodies with caloric clutter, consisting mainly of
fat and sugar. The stuff in our homes becomes too overwhelming to deal with; the increasing weight of our bodies becomes
too much to deal with. One is a mirror of the other.

Every year Americans spend nearly 40 billion dollars on
dieting books and programs, and it's estimated that half of us
diet at some point every year, and yet we keep gaining. What is
the solution? I am convinced that you cannot lose weight, that
you cannot achieve the body and look you desire, if your home is
not clutter-free and organized.

Forget the diet books, the pills, and the gimmicks. Take the
approach I have outlined here for your home and apply it to

your life. Get rid of the clutter that you are buried in. Organize your life and your living space. Start to build your ideal life in your physical space.

Organize your lifestyle around this vision. Schedule reasonable and appropriate exercise. Declutter your kitchen and get rid of the items you no longer use, then organize your pantry and kitchen so they're in alignment with the vision you have for the person you want to be. Discard unhealthy fat- and sugar-laden processed foods. Make space in your refrigerator for fresh vegetables and healthy items. Plan your eating schedule in advance to avoid the last-minute rush for takeout fast food.

Organization is not just about the extra weight of items you have in your home. It's about the total you—including your waistline!

Declutter your parenting

You teach by example. Children are dramatically affected by clutter and disorganization. They are surrounded with too much of everything—except open space in which they can breathe and think. Behavioral problems and learning difficulties often emerge when kids are wildly overstimulated in their clutter-filled homes.

Your kids aren't going to sit you down at the dinner table to confess that the clutter in their home is distressing to them. One mother I worked with, Danielle, swore up and down that her daughter, Casey, was perfectly happy in their apartment, even though Casey had to wind through a maze of boxes to get to her bedroom and did her homework in the bathroom because, she claimed, it was the only place she could concentrate. It's true; Casey was a popular, seemingly well-adjusted teenager. But when she opened the door to their clutter-free home, she burst into tears of relief. I'll never forget what she said: "I never thought I could have this life."

When your home is overrun with clutter, the silent message you are sending to your children is, "I don't like this, but I can't change it." You're telling them, "We can't better ourselves or alter our circumstances." You're saying, "We are all powerless to change things in our lives." You are teaching a message of hopelessness to your children and reinforcing this message every day.

Don't wait until it's too late to teach your children social responsibility, manners, decision-making skills, personal accountability, respect for property, and tolerance of others. All of these fundamental human values are taught from the moment the child becomes aware of his or her surroundings. Create order, establish limits, encourage routines, and foster organization in your home to model the behavior and values you want your children to adopt.

DEAR PETER:

Our son was a seven-year-old nonverbal boy with autism. He disliked his bedroom with all the "boy" decorations everywhere and preferred to sleep in the sparsely decorated guest room. Then we decluttered and reorganized his room so he could find all of his favorite books. The change was immediate. He decided he liked to read and spend time in his own room. What a boon it was to his reading! A few months after the cleanup, he started trying to read his favorite books out loud. Two months after that (with my help), he began to speak single words. People at church would burst into tears every week when they heard him talk.

Since then, he has been lengthening his phrases and singing entire songs. We had been told that children who do not talk by age seven probably never will, so to us this is miraculous. And I'm writing to tell you so because his interest in reading did not blossom until his room was decluttered and became a peaceful place to be.

Thank you.

Declutter your work

When most people talk about organization in the workplace, they think in terms of efficiency, increased productivity, time saved, and money earned. That's all fine and good, but it's a narrow view of what organization will bring to your career. Being organized and decluttered at home means you have less stress in your life and your work. You wake to a house where everything has its place. You can easily find what to wear. Your home gives you a sense of peace and well-being. That's not a bad way to start the day. Once you've allowed yourself to imagine the life you want, you develop a vision for the career you want. When your home is an organized and well-run place, you naturally find it easier to have the clarity and confidence to make that dream a reality.

The organization that you develop at home organically seeps into your working life. You'll find that you aren't distracted by small, routine things. You think more clearly, plan more logically, and solve problems more fluidly. You communicate better with your colleagues. You're less stressed in life and bring less stress into the workplace, no matter if you work in an office, from home, or as a full-time parent. To put it more concretely, the average executive wastes six weeks a year looking for lost and misplaced information and files. *Six weeks!* If your newfound organization buys you that much time, better dial your boss and start talking about that raise and promotion.

ENJOY THE LIFE YOU HAVE

Decluttering and organizing your space inevitably makes you look at how you spend your time. How much of it has been spent acquiring belongings you never use? Recreational shopping—shopping for fun—is a national habit. It makes us feel productive ("We're buying things we need to live life"), successful ("We can afford this—we're doing well"), and in control of our destinies ("If I buy this, my home will be prettier, my wardrobe will be more stylish, I'll finally be happy"). Shopping can easily become a substitute for all kinds of emotional satisfaction. "Retail therapy" may seem like it will ward off loneliness, fear, and dissatisfaction, but it usually leads to credit card bills and more stuff than you have room for. Retail therapy = clutter. There's so much to do beyond spending your life at the mall. Instead of acquiring possessions, we can accumulate life experiences—experiences that breed love and affection.

Outer calm brings inner peace

It comes down to this. Your home is a reflection of who you are. I don't mean this in the sense that you need a showy home to prove to the world how great you are. Your home reflects your inner life. How content you are. How fulfilled you are. How loving and loved you are. Your home is the outward expression of what you value, what you enjoy, and what is important to you.

The road between outer calm and inner peace is a two-way street. Not only is your home the expression of who you really are, but if you don't create a calm and peaceful living space, it is very difficult to grow and develop that inner you. A calm, peaceful, organized home helps keep you focused and in touch with what is important in your life. Living with memories from the past may seem sentimental and romantic, and living for the future may seem ambitious and hopeful. They're both true—

memories are important to all of us, and the drive to build a better future is healthy and productive. But the central purpose of your home should not be to live in a different time and place. You have to enjoy living in the now. It's all you have. When you do that, you can take genuine pleasure in planning the future and remembering the past. You're no longer hiding in one or the other.

It's just enough

As I hope you know by now, my goal in writing this book wasn't to start a white glove movement. I don't have a set idea in my head of how clean your house should be or what a comfortable, happy home looks like. What motivates me are the emotions behind the clutter and the words I hear people use to describe their homes. This book is for the people who are overwhelmed, trapped, suffocating beneath their stuff. This book is for people who think cleaning up is a waste of time, but spend whole weeks of their lives looking for their keys. This book is for people who aren't happy with their lives, but don't know why. This book is for people who feel paralyzed by their own accumulation of goods. This book is for anyone who's ever said, "It's all too much."

For some of you, this book will change everything. For some of you, it will be a first step toward living the life you want. Get there. I know you can.

Acknowledgments

To Ken, who embraces the crazy ride every day and without whom none of this would have been possible.

To my wonderful family—Jim and Kath and my brothers and sisters, Christine, Kay, Michael, Julie, James, and Kelvin—for keeping me grounded and reminding me that they know enough stories to make my life miserable if I step out of line.

To the Team at Evolution Film and Tape—Douglas, Greg, Kathleen, and especially Dean—who were there at the start and continue to smile at the outcome.

To the amazing people at Simon & Schuster / Free Press, especially Suzanne Donahue and Carisa Hays—good friends, trusted advisors, and skilled professionals. A dream team to work with.

To Dean, Elisa, Ken, and Amanda (my muse)—for reading an early draft and giving incisive and valuable feedback. Even when it hurt!

To Hilary—for not running in the opposite direction, and making sure it all made sense.

To Lydia and the team at Paradigm—for helping navigate the small type.

To those brave and wonderful people who have invited me into their lives, seeking advice and direction when it all became too much—this book came from all the lessons you taught me and the infinite capacity you have to surprise me. For that I cannot thank you enough.

About the Author

Part contractor, part therapist, Peter Walsh lives to conquer clutter and help people reorganize their personal spaces. As the organizational guru on TLC's hit show *Clean Sweep*, a regular guest on *The Oprah Winfrey Show*, and the voice of reason on his weekly national radio program, *The Peter Walsh Show*, Peter demonstrates that decluttering is the sure path to a richer, fuller life.

Peter holds a master's degree with a specialty in educational psychology, has worked internationally in corporate training and health promotion, and possesses a keen sense of humor that regularly gets him out of the toughest situations. When not leading those lost in clutter to a happier, less-stressed life, Peter divides his time between Los Angeles and Melbourne, Australia.